My Therapy

My Therapy

Marian Davies

ATHENA PRESS
LONDON

My Therapy
Copyright © Marian Davies 2006

All Rights Reserved

ISBN 1 88401 837 7

First Published 2006 by
ATHENA PRESS
Queen's House, 2 Holly Road
Twickenham TW1 4EG
United Kingdom

Printed for Athena Press

To love, truth and espoir

Chapter 1

I sat in the waiting room of an NHS (National Health Service) psychology centre in a small English town. I was very aware of being an 'ill' patient, contrasting with the well-looking professionals who kept passing me on their way to important meetings (the waiting room was in a corridor). I felt very unimportant and useless. I was thirty-four years old and had tried so hard to construct a meaningful life for myself but was stuck in a miserable marriage, had a failed career behind me, had few friends and no close family. I did have two young children whom I loved immeasurably and who desperately needed a mother capable of looking after them. It was because of my children that I was sitting waiting for my clinical psychologist to call my name.

I had been to a wedding with my family and got so drunk that I wasn't able to look after my children and, during the evening, I had found my four-and-a-half-year-old son wandering about the crowded hotel alone. In the following days, I couldn't get awful images (the strongest being abduction and abuse of my son) out of my head and it was the final event that pushed me into acknowledging that I had 'a mess for a life' and needed help. I went to my GP, asking to be referred to a female clinical psychologist who didn't give pills out, because I had some awareness of psychotherapy through reading books and I had seen my mother ruin her life by relying on an endless supply of pills to get her through each day.

Despite my knowing something about therapy, time was passing at a slow, slow pace in the waiting room and I kept feeling like running from the building, never to return. I couldn't understand why I was so nervous and thought it must be to do with the idea of being in a place that dealt with 'nutters,' yet I knew that mental illness was just another type of illness requiring the help of a doctor.

I was revived from my thoughts by hearing my name being

called and looked up to see a small woman with deep, brown eyes and an open, welcoming smile. I followed her up two flights of stairs then down a narrow, tall, dark corridor and into her room. I could never have imagined how many years ahead I would still be taking those same steps into her warm, institutionalised room. She sat down into her relaxed chair and offered me a similar chair opposite her, again with her wide, warm smile. She asked: 'How can I help you?' and I was surprised to hear a European (possibly French) accent.

I sat timidly on the edge of my chair and asked: 'What therapy do you do?'

She looked slightly taken aback and answered: 'I work psycho-dynamically. Basically, childhood experiences and family relations are explored.'

It's strange how I can vividly remember that, as she was talking, she moved her left index finger in a circle on the arm of her chair. I took this as my cue to give her a brief summary of my family history, beginning at my birth.

'My mother tells me I was born around midday at home with just herself and the midwife in the bedroom, and that I was her easiest birth. My sister, Jocelin (Joss) has told me her version of that day; she's five years older than me and remembers being petrified because of having to make a cup of tea for my mother after my delivery (there was no one else around). I also spoilt her first day at school because my mother was looking after me so the neighbour had to take her and ignored Joss in favour of her own child. I can see that this wasn't a good introduction to Joss and understand how resentment started from that first day. At that time, my mother was thirty-five years old and very alone with her two daughters. She was estranged from her mother, hardly saw her sisters, her father was dead and she had few friends. My mother had problems looking after us and before I was six years old I had been to several carers, foster homes and nurseries and, between the ages of seven and thirteen, was sent to boarding school.

'My father was not there on the day of my birth and, for the whole of my childhood, he missed my birthday because I was born in the holidays. The holidays were always spent in France with his "real" family. My father had three families: his "legitimate" one (wife and three children), his first illegitimate one (my mother, older sister and younger brother) and his second illegitimate one (lover and one child). So I was my mother's and father's second illegitimate daughter, but my father's fifth child and third daughter. It probably seems old fashioned to be going on about legitimacy but, when I was a child, it was still not widely accepted.

'My father was born in Paris, an only child to a working class family. His father was a train driver and his mother a seamstress. I know very little about them because they were never told of our existence but my half-sister (I am very particular about referring to my siblings in terms of their "full" or "half" relationship to me) tells me that his father spent a lot of time drinking in the local café and his mother adored her son, breastfeeding him until he was at least two years old. My father married soon after the war and came to England as a French teacher in a northern English town and, apparently, he worked very hard to become a lecturer in a local college, which later became a university. His working life was a strict pattern of being in England during the college/University term times, then heading off to Paris every holiday with his "real" family to spend time with their relations, to work as a lecturer and to write books on French literature. He never lived with us and we never had any part in his holidays. It's very hard to talk about this without feeling gnawing bitterness edging up my throat. No holidays were ever spent with my dad for the whole of my childhood yet during term-time he visited us when he could. Mum can't really remember when he first saw me, or even heard of my birth, as there was no phone.'

It's amazing how much information can be given over in only fifty minutes when only one person is talking and the other listening. By the end I was crying, saying: 'I can't understand because my father said he loved me.' I looked across at the brown-eyed woman (I didn't know what else to call her) and she was saying: 'Well, that's a lot to have told me,' to which I responded by asking: 'Can you help me?'

'Yes, I can see you weekly for an hour,' she replied.

'How long will it take?'

She smiled seriously. 'We're talking about months.' I left in such a whirl of feelings; euphoria at being listened to, surprise at having focussed on my relationship with my father, intrigue about my doctor's background and the feeling that I was already looking forward to my appointment next week. I was bursting to tell her my whole history and, as soon as I was back in that chair for my next hour, I began to tell her more.

'My mother had often told me of her childhood, that her mother should never have married her father and that she was very erratic in moods, shouting very suddenly then being exuberantly happy. My great grandmother was a wealthy, upper-class woman; her husband was a member of the England Cricket Team and longed to have sons but they had four daughters, my grandmother being the third daughter. They were reared in typical British upper-class manner by nannies and hardly saw their parents. My grandmother, a gregarious "actress type" was married at just nineteen to a solicitor, not quite her class but lots of men had been killed in the First World War so, as my mother always explained: "There was limited choice." She had children soon after marriage and desperately wanted sons but she had three daughters (my mother was her second daughter) and one son who died at birth. Because she was so distraught, he was "replaced" secretly by an adopted son. She dressed her first two daughters as boys as often as possible in a game that they learned to enjoy because their mother seemed happy but, when her third daughter was born, she could no longer play these "boy" games and her anger became targeted at her three daughters, particularly at her third. One story tells of her holding her third two-or-three-year-old daughter over a high bridge threatening to drop her.

'The Second World War came and, because they lived in London, gave the perfect excuse for the daughters to be sent to the country to be with their grandmother, but she couldn't manage the three of them so they were sent to boarding school for the rest of the war. Occasionally, my mother would go and stay with her mother and brother in London and, because of the bombing, at night they would have to sleep in the cellar. Her mother slept on a thick mattress with her son while my mother had thin cushions and was so angry she pushed them aside so that her back was in continuous contact with the cold concrete floor. She hoped her mother would notice or that she would get ill so that her mother would have to look after her. My mother did start to become ill with deep, low backache but her mother didn't notice. Around this time my grandmother met her "true love", as the story is told, so she did the unthinkable by becoming pregnant to her lover, forcing my grandfather to divorce her, and she finally had a son who lived, at which point she started to withdraw completely from her daughters' and adopted son's lives.

'Her new husband was a wealthy landowner and she moved to his mansion and erased her past. My mother always maintained that she was relieved to be out of her mother's life and would occasionally visit her father who lived by himself but he died soon after my sister was born. My mother was the "cleverest" daughter, excelling at science and literature; she chose to study to be a doctor because she "wanted to help people who were suffering". She managed the first three years of being a student doctor, but, when they began hospital rounds, the pain in her lower back meant that she simply couldn't remain standing and she would take to her bed for days with her "bad back". She had to withdraw from her studies and, as her grandmother and aunt had taken on the role of parents, they sent her to various private back specialists who could find nothing physically wrong so they then sent her to a private mental hospital where she was given "twilight sleep treatment".

'At the end of her treatment, she moved to London and looked at careers in drama and speech therapy. The course she chose was speech therapy because she particularly liked the principle. Although she was still plagued by her "bad back" (as she always refers to it), she completed the training and started a job in the north of England, where she met my father at a French literature class he was teaching.'

This hour passed very rapidly and suddenly the kind, brown-eyed lady was saying: 'Let's continue next week, shall we?' I looked at my watch and saw we'd gone five minutes over and I felt that I'd somehow done something wrong. I left feeling like I'd stopped mid-sentence and spent all the next week waiting to continue.

'The first five months of my life were really some sort of paradise for me; breastfed on demand, no tight swaddling, mother cuddling and kissing me and singing to me or reciting poetry and hearing classical music (which my mother loves). Mum was also very conscious of nature and would often, in those first few months, put me naked in the garden to feel the grass and watch the leaves of the trees sway gently in the warm summer breezes. Father would "pop in" every weekday after work for an hour (he hadn't told his wife about us so we were banished from his life at weekends) and he would sometimes also arrive unexpectedly in the day when he had no lectures.

'Mum had to go back to work when I was five months old and, from one day to the next, I was in free, loving arms then thrown into the rigorous routine of full-time day nursery where bottles were given strictly every four hours, nappies changed with disgusted faces staring down and enforced sleeps in the afternoons. I have dream-like memories of the shock at being thrust into this so abruptly, no preparation, no gentle introduction, just suddenly finding myself in a completely alien environment. I can still feel the bewilderment, particularly at the feeling of the hard rubber teat thrust into my mouth, with foul-tasting liquid sticking in my throat. I remember feeling such indignation, rage and confusion and, although my mother offered me her breast in the evenings, I could only turn away because I was so upset my hunger had vanished. My mother does remember me turning away and has said: "Yes, it was odd because you just seemed to lose interest in breastfeeding."'

At this point, I asked my therapist: 'Do you really think that my memory is real or is it my imagination?'

'I'm sure that this is how you experienced these events,' she replied quietly and slowly.

'In the evenings, after work and at the weekends, my mother would sometimes go out, leaving me alone with Joss. Joss remembers these times clearly because she has often said to me, with blame towards me in her voice: "I felt terrified when left to care for you." I can see that she had had five reasonably quiet years with my mother (my mother would spend her evenings playing with her and sometimes take her to the theatre) and had the little time that my father gave to us for herself. Added to all this, my mother decided to move house at about this time and became pregnant with my "real" brother when I was thirteen months old. The chaos seeped into my care and, before my brother was born, I had nearly lost my right eye through falling out of my high chair and ended up in hospital having my stomach pumped out because I'd eaten Mummy's iron tablets.

'My mother used to visit her grandmother regularly in the school holidays but she could only take one child, as that's all her gran said she could manage, yet she lived in a large farmhouse in acres of land with a cook, cleaners and gardeners. When I was about sixteen months old my mother and Joss visited my mother's grandmother in the summer holidays and the neighbour, who usually looked after me, was going to be away so my mother advertised in the local press for someone to look after her toddler for a week. A woman answered the ad, spoke to mum on the phone and, despite having never met her before, my mother dropped me at her house on my own and left me for a week (I could barely talk and was still in nappies). I only became aware of this because, when I was sixteen years old, I started to have strange images in my head about being in a house alone with a woman doing awful things to me and the images and sensations had an odd quality in that I was a very little girl with a nappy on experiencing terror. I asked my mother if I had ever been alone with a woman at such a young age so she told me, in an unemotional voice, how she had found someone to look after me. She also said: "Yes, I left you for a few days, or was it a week? It's funny but I do remember leaving you on your own with a skinny woman but I can't remember why and I do remember feeling peculiar but I can't remember when I picked you up."'

I stop and the room is very silent, my therapist simply sitting silently looking gently at me. The silence seems interminable then

13

suddenly my brown-eyed friend is saying: 'Let's continue next week, shall we?' I was still immersed in my early childhood and continued in our next session.

'My brother Raymond (Ray) was born at home in the new house and I and my sister were sent to be looked after by neighbours. The midwife left, my mother was thirty-six years old and alone with her three children. Ray was born in the Christmas holidays so my father didn't see him until he returned from Paris. I knew I loved Ray. I adored his cuddly body and loved to lie next to him, kissing his soft face, smelling his sweet, gentle breath. I loved him so much I wanted to make everything good for him. I tried to soothe him when he cried by stroking his lovely soft head but when he didn't stop I would cry too and run to find Mummy, who seemed distant and helpless. Occasionally, she would manage to revive and sing her old songs and read stories to us but often she just managed to feed us, Ray with his bottle, me and Joss so often with boiled eggs and yummy soldiers.

'I continued to go to the nursery and Joss to school. When Mum went back to work Ray joined me at the nursery. Mum tells me of having to get up in the freezing cold (no central heating) and crying with cold and backache as she lit the two coal fires, then getting all of us ready for the day.'

I then returned to my memories of the week I spent in a woman's care alone at sixteen months old.

'I started to have vivid flashes in my teens of a woman giving me a bath but holding my head under water too long, until I start to squirm and struggle for breath.

'She holds me until my lungs start to burn, until my strength starts to wane, then she lets me up and smiles and laughs and shampoos my hair then puts me under again, saying my hair is extra dirty and this just seems to go on and on without a break. When I'm out of the bath, she puts my nappy on and sticks the pin in my thigh while looking directly into my eyes saying: "Sorry, did I hurt you?" Then she puts me to bed but she tells me to "get in bed," then to "get out of bed" and she does this repeatedly until I'm really flagging then she speeds up. I never know when she'll stop. Mummy phones up. The woman stands over me looking like a giant. I have no words. Mummy keeps talking. I have no words and as I start to cry the giant woman takes the heavy black handset off me.'

I asked my therapist: 'Do you think this really happened to me?'
'Of course. Why would those things be in your head?'
'Why would someone want to do that to me?'
'It wasn't your fault; some people are just very nasty.'

'The feeling of having no words is so strong. It's like I have all the images in my head but I cannot translate them into words and I am paralysed by my smallness and terror. I have vivid physical feelings of standing holding the heavy phone to my ear, my hand can hardly hold it, and looking up at this huge lady, and feeling so tiny and helpless. What did she get out of treating me like that? I can hardly communicate the terrible feeling of complete humiliation and powerlessness at being ordered to hop in and out of bed just on her whim. I am completely in her control and that means that I, Marian, ceased to exist. I can only understand this by interpreting the feelings through my adult communicating brain. It's as if I'm explaining what happened to the child part of myself who doesn't understand. I can't really begin to explain what it feels like to be taken to the brink of death by drowning, repeatedly, by a smiling woman. I think that during those events I somehow "shut down".'

I left that session feeling desperately panicky, finally realising that the awful woman had existed for real and not just in my nightmares. I didn't really know how to cope with the idea of this having really happened to me and I was very confused. I managed to drive myself home while still shaking with the full realisation of having an awareness of such terror; I could still feel the panic, utter confusion and such a desperate feeling of complete aloneness that I just didn't want to exist. Thoughts of suicide had been with me for as long as I could remember; why was life so fucking hard?

I arrived home to the small terraced house that I shared with my husband, daughter and son. My husband, Simon, was home because he'd been unemployed for the previous seven months. We had been married for twelve years and met at poly where we both studied for a degree. We were quite an 'odd' couple because a few months after we met we moved into a flat and hardly mixed with any other students. It wasn't particularly my choice to isolate myself but I was painfully shy and Simon disliked parties, pubs and so on, basically any event that was noisy and crowded he avoided. We did both get good degrees and moved to a university where we studied for PhDs and again we had not made any friends. During my PhD I had our daughter (Sophie), which was such a wonderfully absorbing experience for me that I managed to ignore my loneliness and isolation.

However, Simon's relationship to Sophie began to worry me when she was about eighteen months old. It began with one incident. Sophie was being noisy and boisterous at a barbeque we had been invited to by a friend I had made through mother and toddler groups. We asked her to stop what she was doing but, as children do, she continued. Suddenly, Simon jumped from his chair and grabbed Sophie by the shoulders, lifting her into the air, and, putting his face very close to hers, he said in a nasty, low, angry tone: 'I told you to stop'. In that instant the whole atmosphere in the garden became tense and silent; the other adults staring at Simon and Sophie.

After we left I confronted him, we had a huge argument, and there were no more outbursts until I was pregnant with our son. His family history is sad because his father died suddenly when he was nine and his mother spent most of the next years staving off money problems and having several boyfriends so Simon had a series of substitute dads from the age of ten (his mother had no close brothers and saw little of her father). His story becomes more complicated as he was his parents' second boy when they had desperately wanted girls and he felt that his mother and father were often horrible to him for not having been a girl.

His mother often joked about putting him in his pram at the end of the garden because he screamed for food all the time. His father was particularly strict with ridiculous rules like: 'At the end of a meal the last forkful has to be the size of a penny', which meant that Simon spent his whole meal worried about the size of his last forkful. Simon also told me that, shortly before his father's death, his father had put him over his knee and smacked his bare bottom (he had not been quiet when his parents had told him to) while his mother, brother and younger sister were in the next room. I knew that his background must have something to do with his angry outburst and, although I did often want to leave him, I had no family or friends I could go to and no job or money. Also, Simon was great at taking the children out for walks and bike rides, which they loved.

My whole focus in life was trying to give my children the secure environment they needed to grow into strong adults, yet it was so hard to achieve, particularly as I was often ill and so tired that I could hardly manage to get up some mornings. I had tried to develop a career after my PhD but lacked enough confidence to pursue research and lecturing (I found public speaking unbearably difficult) and I had ended up in a couple of part-time temporary jobs in local government offices that didn't lead on to anything. Added to my career problems were Simon's work-related difficulties, because he had been applying for jobs in his field of research all over the world for several years before he became unemployed, which had meant that I kept thinking we would be moving from our area.

Events in my life seemed to come together in such a way that it became very difficult to manage to live without misery. I was at a loss to know what the causes were of my failure to create a life with a reasonably happy family, meaningful work (that would give me desperately needed money) and supportive friends. I knew that images and feelings from my childhood still haunted me and might have something to do with my failures, so I was hoping that the therapy would give me some answers and show me the way to a fulfilled life.

Chapter 2

It was as if I'd been waiting all my life to be able to tell my story to someone who would take the time to listen and the pace of my therapy settled into a pattern of slowly telling her my story, moving backwards, forwards and sideways through my life; one week I would be talking about my early childhood, the next my teenage years, then another week current life events would be discussed. My hour with my therapist (my favourite person for several years to come) was fixed to each Thursday at 11 a.m. So, at about 10 a.m. I would drive to the 'nutter building,' as I joked with Simon, to be there about five to ten minutes before my appointment. It became the most important event for me each week and the hours between seemed to drag. Today I was telling her about living with my mother as a teenager. My heart was pounding and I felt sick.

'I am about fourteen years old, living with my mother and brother, and it is like living in a grotty bedsit. I do all my own washing and ironing and make most of my own meals, which often consist of Vesta curries, meat pies bought from the local shop and lots of pasta with tomato sauce and grated cheddar cheese. The kitchen is usually a disgusting mess; my mother cannot do the washing up on a daily basis and has two huge sinks where all the dishes pile up. She soaks them in water and, after a few days, the water is a whitish, thickish foul-smelling liquid that has to be drained out before the dishes can be washed. I often do the washing-up and tidy the kitchen and Ray never does, which is a source of lots of arguments that Mum never tries to sort out. The kitchen also has an infestation of cockroaches that are all over the floor at night and are revolting especially when walking across them at night, hearing the crunching, and then seeing the dead ones in the morning.

'My mother does do food shopping but often leaves it at the shops for Ray or me to pick up. She just buys the basics and lets us take care of ourselves; she often cooks some soup or boiled eggs for herself, carefully lays the meal out on a tray and then, sitting up in bed, eats in her bedroom while either listening to the radio (usually Radio 3 or Radio 4) or watching TV. She also has a habit of going to the fishmonger for a bag of fish heads that she boils for ages, which absolutely stinks the house out (she completely ignores our protests about the smell) and she then lets the fish heads cool and carefully removes all the remaining fish. This meal is for the cat and it looks to me as if she takes more trouble feeding the cat than Ray and me.

'In fact, it appears as if she is hardly aware of our presence in her house. She also seems oblivious to the inside of the house which is in a horrible mess; the walls are covered with ripped wallpaper and we have no carpets on the stairs and hallway. The kitchen and dining room have patches of old lino on the floor that slip about and the bedrooms have rough cord carpets. I try to persuade Mum to get some flooring for the stairs and hall and plead with her to get a carpet. She gets really angry with me saying: "Carpets in halls get disgustingly dirty and I'm not having one" but she does go to buy some lino for the halls, which lies rolled up in the downstairs hallway until I lay it myself (badly). I then decide the only option with the stairs is to paint them, which I do, in dark navy blue gloss (it must have been infuriating for the neighbours having to put up with the noise from the painted wooden stairs).

'The one good thing about the house is that it is always very warm because my mother hates the cold as it's bad for her back. We have full central heating plus gas fires in the kitchen/dining room, in the two downstairs rooms and the upstairs large bedroom (which is the TV room for Ray and me). The evenings are often spent with Ray watching TV in the living room upstairs but are marred by the fact that we sometimes have terrible fights over which channel to watch on the TV, which can be quite frightening and noisy, yet my mother rarely intervenes. Occasionally, I go to watch TV with my mother in her bedroom and she's often watching documentaries about either the genocide of the Second World War or victims of torture in countries with dictatorships or victims of violence and abuse in this country. She also has the *Guardian* delivered daily and, again, focuses on the articles about injustice and torture (basically any news that is about our capacity for inhumanity) and she carefully cuts any "interesting" articles out and piles them on top of the years of articles she has already. She then does the crossword, which she is determined to complete (it may take up to a few days), and she eagerly sends off in the hope of winning a prize; getting the finished crossword into the post is an important task for her to accomplish. She also usually has a novel that she is reading; books are a great love of hers which provide an additional distraction and help her to fill her days and nights (she often reads late into the night).

'Her daily routine involves so much of her attention that she doesn't have much time left for us (or the house). Sometimes we would talk about her life and she would say that she wished she'd never met my father to which I would reply: "But I wouldn't have been born (or Ray and Joss)". She would look directly at me with a broad smile and say in a superior tone: "But I would have had other children to a different man." She seemed to take some pleasure in making my existence easily replaceable. At other times she would say to me with a desperate look on her face: "I would kill myself if it weren't for you, Ray and Joss", which would make me feel suffocated with guilt for ruining her life because she often said, in a voice leaden with doom: "Once you have children your life changes for ever."

'I had recently started a new school and my routine begins by waking in the morning to a breakfast, on my own or with Ray, of one cup of coffee and walking to the bus stop with Mark and Rob (a couple of lads who live in my street). My mother decided that Ray should go to the local boys school (why, with her adamant liberal socialist ideals, is unfathomable) and so we go our separate ways to school. Soon after the autumn term begins, I find that the results from the tests I'd had in each subject (to assess the set that I should be put in) last term were abysmal so I am deemed "not academic" (thick) and put in the lowest sets in all subjects except French and am also put in cookery and needlework classes. I don't bother to tell my mother because she rarely asks any questions about school or schoolwork. It's interesting because this helps me to understand that a very confusing aspect of our relationship is an almost complete lack of her interest in me and my life. She hardly ever asks me any questions about any part of my life and she later justifies this by saying: "I wanted you to find your own way of doing things."

'The reality is that she is chronically depressed and never gets any help for this problem because she persistently presents doctors with her "back problems". She visits the doctor regularly with occasional visits to a new specialist who might hopefully offer her a panacea for her overwhelming pain. The doctors prescribe for her endless pain-relieving drugs, which she takes throughout each and every day, and they must have affected her thought processes; basically she is out of her head everyday on a cocktail of "pain killers" (life destroyers?). She has managed to get a home help to clean the house but the pattern is always the same; they come for a while and are "fantastic" then she decides they have a particularly annoying fault and sacks them. She won't listen to me as I plead her to keep a home help (the Social Services eventually stop sending her any other home helps) and the house slides, yet again, into filth and chaos.

My father lives in the same town and we see him almost daily (except during the holidays) and he often brings food with him, usually steaks and sometimes fish (giving us much-needed protein for our growing teenage bodies).

'My father lives in the "middle class suburbs" and Celine (my half-sister who is a couple of years older than me) goes to her local school full of "academic" children and is in all the top sets. I cannot understand how my father allowed our education to be so inadequate compared to his "legitimate" children and how he allowed us to lived in such a dump while he and his family live in such a clean, tidy house in a calm and green suburb. His house is a 1930s brick semi on a tree-lined road with a large, comforting garden, although Celine said to me later: "We would have had a bigger detached house if it hadn't been for you," so the house is obviously small for his status as a senior university lecturer (a couple of years later to be a professor).

'I have such ambivalent feelings for my father because if he didn't show us his house or take us out we would never have any relief from our grim surroundings because my mother never takes us out; she sticks to her relentless routine, of pills and bed everyday, for so long. But did my father partly cause her to live like this by never leaving his wife? It's so complicated to sort out in my head and I swing from feeling so angry with both my parents to feeling grateful for the care that they do manage to give me because without it I would not have any possibility of survival.

On a Friday evening, my father often takes us out to the local Chinese restaurant and sometimes, if my mother "is up to it," she comes too, but when she's there complains about how "uncomfortable" the hard chairs are for her back and, occasionally, she lets out a loud groan of "pain", which sounds orgasmic and it feels as if the entire restaurant becomes silent as people stare at us. My father tries to ameliorate the atmosphere by getting us to laugh with his jokes: "Have I told you of the joke about bread and butter?"

'We pretend we've never heard it before and reply "no" then he smilingly says: "I'd better not, you might spread it!" and we all end up in fits of giggles. At the weekends my father regularly takes us either to the beach or the countryside for walks and Celine sometimes comes with him and even, occasionally, his wife.'

My therapist sat silently while gently looking at me then said: 'Your mother and father didn't seem to have the capacity to think of your needs and this must have been very hard for you.' It was the first time I'd heard someone talk about my needs and I felt a mixture of rage and desperate sadness. The next few weeks continued with my teenage years.

'Soon after starting my new school I make a friend with a girl called Jackie (from the year above) and begin to spend most of my time out of school with her. She has a youth club next to her house, which runs a disco each Friday night so I, most Fridays, go directly to her house after school (she lives about twenty minutes away from me by car) and have tea that her mother has prepared. We then get ready together and later I return to spend the night at her house. I love dancing and look forward to the weekly disco but also her mother is very kind and her house is beautifully tidy and clean but cold, as they don't have central heating. Jackie's parents are divorced and her mother remarried to a reasonably friendly man who seems quite happy to include me in their family. On Saturdays, we go shopping into town and then come back to my house for the evening, where we make tea together and then invite "the boys" (Rob, Chris, Mark and Russ) over to drink and listen to music in my bedroom. Jackie then goes home on the Sunday morning. Jackie's not a regular drinker or smoker, which reduces my drunkenness, though I smoke every day (I had started smoking regularly when at my first boarding school at seven years old).

'During this time, we meet some older boys at the club and we both like Ian who is quite good-looking. He asks me to meet him on a Saturday evening at the park and I am quite excited and nervous because I really like him. We meet several times before he starts to want to kiss me and although I find him very exciting to be with, whenever we kiss I feel sick and, when he starts to breathe heavily, I freeze and become rigid. I am so confused because I do like him so much. He then gives up on me and goes out with Jackie for a while, which makes me feel so useless; why can't I just enjoy kissing and cuddling like others? Jackie then starts to go out with Chris and they spend a lot of time at my house "cuddling" in a corner while I get drunk with Rob, Russ and Mark. Jackie then persuades me to give Patrick a go, even though I think he's ugly, and she arranges for us to meet at Chris's house one Saturday when his parents are out. She even persuades me that I should let Patrick sleep with me while she sleeps with Chris. I don't know whether she is a virgin (I am) but I allow her to set it all up because I think that maybe "going all the way" is the key to me enjoying it. The evening comes and I'm feeling very nervous but we have some cider and beer, which we all drink, then Patrick leads me to the bathroom where he has laid a towel on the floor, and tells me to take my trousers and knickers off. I lay down on the towel, naked from the waist down, and he lies on top of me; soon it's all over and all I feel is pain and disgust. We go back into the living room where Chris has slept with Jackie and she has a big grin on her face and says to me: "It's great, isn't it?" I force myself to smile and nod, and then say I have to get home as I feel like I'm going to be sick when I look at Patrick.'

I looked up into those deep, brown eyes and I thought I saw sadness and anger. She said: 'That must have been very distressing for you.' I continued with some of my sexual history.

'When I'm about twelve years old and home from boarding school for the Christmas holidays, a new person is staying at our house (my mother often has other single parents and their children staying with her). The man is Joss's new boyfriend who is very old for her (about fifteen years older than her) and is ugly and is homeless so is "dossing at our place". Joss is very open about her sexual activities, deep kisses him in my vicinity (actually standing right next to me) and has noisy late sessions behind closed doors. Joss goes back to school before Ray and me, and her boyfriend spends the time she's at school with me, giving me booze, fags and pot. I quite like the attention but when he starts to kiss me I feel sick and scared but I can't seem to move or say anything and he then removes my knickers and "feels in me" and "sucks at me," all in Joss's bedroom. That night, I awake in the middle of the night and vomit all over the floor and, as I share a bedroom with Ray, he goes and gets Mum who does clean it up, saying: "You've obviously picked up a bug." Joss's boyfriend then keeps trying to get me on my own but I manage to avoid him by staying with Ray in our bedroom playing board games. My mother has given me a diary for Christmas and I write it down which makes me feel less scared.'

My therapist asked if I told anybody because: 'What happened to you was sexual abuse.' I was stunned to hear those words and said nothing except: 'It made me feel so sick.' I was ready now to tell her about being raped when I was fourteen years old, a few weeks after I had lost my virginity.

'I don't spend quite as much time with Jackie any more, after the incident with Patrick and I start to hang out with Rob and Mark and a girl called Bev from the youth club. On a Friday I go to the disco with Bev now (I don't really like her but there isn't anybody else) and sometimes I go to her house to get ready but only occasionally stay the night because I don't like her mother. At the youth club, I've met a boy called Dave who flirts with me and I quite like him but he's seeing someone else. One Saturday, around this time, Bev calls me and says that Dave is having a party at his house as his parents are away and Rob and Mark are already there, so I quickly get ready and walk round to his house (it takes about twenty minutes). They are all in his living room, drinking and smoking, and it seems quite fun but soon after Bev calls to me from upstairs and beckons me to come up, saying that she wants to tell me something.

'I go upstairs and she calls me into the bathroom and she asks me to do up her bra as it's come undone, which I willingly do, and, as I open the door to come out of the bathroom, Rob, Mark and Dave are standing in the doorway. Dave tells them to grab me and, with them, pushes me into a small box bedroom with a single bed. I cannot understand what they are doing and think it must be some sort of joke but they then push me on to the floor and hold me down while they start to pull my trousers and knickers off and I am struggling to stop them, occasionally managing to grab my trousers back up and Bev is watching from the doorway.

'I am so completely taken aback and beg them: "Please, please don't do it", and they stop and, for a second, I think it's over but Dave insists they carry on and when I am naked from the waist he orders them to leave. He is quite a tall, muscular young man and I cannot push him away and by this time I am frozen with rigidity and can hardly speak. He forces me to lie on the bed and quickly opens his trousers and then lies on top of me but I have my legs firmly closed and say in a barely audible whisper: "I don't want to do it", but he prises my legs apart and rapes me. Then, as he's pulling closed his trousers and, walking towards the door to leave, he turns to me, smiling at me and saying in a glittering tone: 'You enjoyed that really, didn't you?"

'I am feeling very odd (strangely floaty) and shakily get dressed and go downstairs to the living room where Bev, Rob, and Mark are watching TV (Dave is not there). I talk to them as if nothing has happened and sit down to watch TV. Then something really strange happens; Bev starts to shake all over and cry and says she can't breathe and it becomes so bad that Mark calls for an ambulance. It's now very weird as the ambulance men come in and check her over and then take her away in a wheelchair yet I am the one who has just suffered a shockingly degrading and humiliating ordeal at the hands of my "friends".

'Rob and Mark then walk me home while both joking and talking excessively, to which I respond mechanically. I feel very odd, sort of removed from everything, for quite a few weeks, yet my mother doesn't notice. I can't tell anybody what has happened because I don't know what to make of it and somehow feel like I was to blame because I flirted with Dave though how it happened, being set up by Bev, Rob and Mark, feels like an act of vengeance yet I never significantly harmed any of them.'

My therapist sat silently looking at me with her sad eyes. 'That must have been a big shock to you.'

'Why would they do that to me?' I asked her very quietly.

She answered slowly and deliberately. 'The reasons why people do terrible things can be complicated but for you it's important to know that you did not deserve to be treated that way and some of the reasons for you are that you were very vulnerable because your parents did not look after you properly.' I didn't acknowledge what she said and rushed on.

'I refuse to speak to Bev ever again and I don't have much contact with Rob or Mark, though they try to be excessively nice to me at the school bus stop which, I guess, does show some remorse on their part. The Christmas holidays arrive soon after and I spend most of my time in my room listening to music and drinking and smoking. I asked my mother for Tchaikovsky's *Swan Lake* (it's the only classical music I know the name of) for a Christmas present, which she gives to me, and spend a lot of time listening to parts of this music, which sometimes makes me feel wonderfully floaty, like flying into the sky far away from everything, and at others, a desperately sad hopelessness that I can barely tolerate.

'I do begin to feel less odd and by the time I go back to school tell myself that I'm going to try really hard to do well in my subjects. I tell my father that I need some help with maths so he gets me a tutor who comes to see me weekly after school. I also endeavour to get my homework done, particularly in biology which I find relatively easy.'

I left the session feeling bruised and ill and for a while I couldn't stop thinking about how and why I was raped. I was in regular contact with my mother by phone (she lived with Joss and her family) and in a call soon after this I said to my mother: 'Do you know I was raped when I was fourteen years old?'

She replied in the most infuriating way: 'Are you sure?'

This sent me into a shouting rage and I screamed down the phone: 'How do you think I would not know if I was raped?'

'You can't blame me for it, can you?'

At this point I slammed the phone down.

My relationship with my mother was characterised by her making comments that made me feel either numb or demented with anger. This had been so for as long as I could remember. I had only just begun to think about her effects on me because I had usually thought of her in terms of her being ill. All through my life she had had her "bad back", meaning that she couldn't work (was on disability benefit most of her working life) and would spend most of her days lying in bed. My most common thoughts when with her were being overwhelmed with feeling terribly sorry for her and wanting to make her pain go away. I was now beginning to question what her illness was and why she hadn't manage to care for me enough to be concerned about my daily welfare and the quality of my education (she was educated to degree level). What life did she imagine I was going to have? Did she ever think about what my future might be? I don't have any memories of her asking me what I would do when I grew up, what type of house I would like to live in or what man I might like to marry.

Chapter 3

I had been going to therapy for a few months when, as I was driving to my session, I suddenly heard a voice in my head saying: 'She's not there.' I thought this ridiculous but I couldn't lose my feeling of panic at the thought that she might not be there. As I told the receptionist my name, she went very red and said: 'I'm so sorry but Vida is not here today because she's ill. We tried to phone you but we couldn't find your phone number.' I was stunned and stood there feeling as if the bottom had fallen out of my world. How could she not be there and did I really hear a voice telling me this fact? I stumbled to my car and drove home feeling very alone and frightened. The next couple of weeks passed very slowly until I finally received a letter telling me of my next appointment.

I was so relieved to be sitting opposite my warm doctor friend and she was apologising to me.

'I'm so sorry that you came when I was ill. It shouldn't have happened and I've made sure that your home contact details are on file so it won't happen again.' This was a new experience for me; someone apologising so sincerely for having hurt me. I was rendered speechless for quite a while and it was the beginning of me spending time in my sessions in a complete silence that was only occasionally broken by Dr Vida. To break the awkward silence, I started to tell her about Simon and my children.

'Simon has been unemployed for over a year despite applying for a job nearly every month and trying to start his own consultancy. This has put enormous strain on our finances and we're virtually broke with debts piling up on our credit cards. His relationship with the children is sometimes great but there is a perceptible atmosphere of tension because Simon tends to explode with anger at some slight error the children may make which is particularly bad around mealtimes. If the children don't finish what is on their plate or touch food they don't eat he will shout and bang his fists on the table and force them to eat the food they have touched, though this only happens sporadically because I usually refuse to allow him to do this and when I stand up to him, he runs out of the house slamming doors and banging light switches so they break. I used to try to hide the fact that I'd thrown food away the children hadn't eaten but sometimes he would find it in the bin and shout at me. Added to this is the fact that Adrian is very skinny and refuses to eat regularly so sometimes, because I know he hasn't eaten for quite some time, I have to sit him down and say: "You cannot go to play unless you eat your sandwich." This makes me very confused as to what is the right thing to do. Simon also has rules that must not be crossed: Sophie is not to be one minute late when coming in from playing (she is about eight years old) and doors have to be closed without banging them. He can become obsessed with one particular aspect of their behaviour and be relentless in his implementation of his new rule. I challenge him but my parenting is problematic in that I can't stick to rules and find it difficult to say "no" to our children. On one occasion Adrian, at about five years old, said to me after a vicious argument with Simon about rules: "Daddy spends his time putting pain into me and you take it out." It has got to the point where Simon has little to do with the children in the house (he still takes them out to the playground and for bike rides) and I am very tired of doing the bedtime routine every evening because Adrian says he doesn't want Daddy to put him to bed.'

Dr Vida intervened, saying: 'You must take turns in putting the children to bed and stick to it'.

'How do I refuse Adrian's tears for me?' I asked.

'Make a list and explain to him that Mummy and Daddy are taking turns and let him read the list each evening' Vida replied confidently. She looked at her watch (I hated this moment) and said her usual ending phrase: 'Shall we continue next week?'

When back at home, I told Simon what Vida had suggested we do about Adrian's bedtime routine and was quite surprised because he was enthusiastic and, when Adrian arrived home from school we wrote the list together. The week passed and I couldn't wait to see Vida to tell her how well her idea worked, but as I was about to leave the phone rang and it was her secretary saying to me: 'Sorry but Vida is ill so we'll have to cancel your session for today and we'll contact you when she's better.' I was gutted but barely aware of the mixture of feelings associated with her not being there for me. I knew that I was fascinated by Vida and was intensely curious about her life and relationships and wondered what her illness was but I hadn't had the courage to ask her secretary. I had found out that Vida was a Jewish Israeli with two children, living in the city close to my village. I waited for the post each day, hoping that the letter would arrive with my next appointment. It finally arrived, and I was once again in my cosy space with my warm, soft-smelling favourite woman and she started by apologising for being ill the previous week. I found her saying sorry awkward and mumbled: 'That's OK', and as I was bursting to tell her how her suggestion for the bedtime list had been so successful, rushed into saying how 'Adrian goes to the list each evening and tells us whose turn it is and it's fantastic because I've recently heard them laughing together when Simon is reading the bedtime story.'

Vida smiled broadly. 'I'm so pleased that things are a bit easier for you.'

I then quickly asked: 'What's it like putting your children to bed?' She was silent for quite a while so I said: 'You do have children, don't you?'

'Yes, yes I do but I wondered why you asked.' I felt ridiculous and sat in silence for some considerable time before returning to my relationship with Simon.

'I don't have sex with Simon very often; in fact, sometimes we go for months without sex. We don't even sleep in the same bed. Soon after we started living together, Simon started to sleep on the sofa because I prevented him from sleeping by trying to cuddle him while asleep. Since then, we've slept in single beds either side by side or, when we're annoying each other, at each end of the room. This has been a sadness to me but doesn't seem to bother Simon who simply says: 'It's due to physical incompatibility while sleeping.' Sex has never been easy for me and before I met Simon I'd had a regular boyfriend for four years and I had not enjoyed sex; it was something I put up with to keep him as a boyfriend. When I met Simon, I felt much more but it wasn't until we'd been living together for some months that I had my first orgasm. Even then, sex was not something that ever came spontaneously to us but, because I experienced some pleasure with Simon, I accepted it. As the years passed, we had sex less and less. We often talked about it and had read books and tried various techniques but after a while we slipped back into avoiding having sex. I didn't know who avoided it more, and with all our other problems, we had sort of come to terms with it. I knew that I was different from my sister because she had regularly had noisy sex with her boyfriends and, later, with her husband, in my vicinity. Also, I had various friends in my teens that seemed to think sex was great.'

Vida asked: 'Have you considered marital therapy?'

'We tried that a couple of years ago but it didn't have much impact.'

She reassured me that 'problems can take time to sort out.'

'I just don't know what to do; we're on benefits, using the credit cards to pay off our loans and we're about to reach our credit limits. Simon has occasional jobs through his consultancy, but it's not enough to pay our credit cards. I'm so frightened that we'll lose the house and can't bear the thought of what it would do to our children.'

My therapist looked slightly uneasy (this is not usual) and told me: 'You must go and get some advice. Have you tried the Citizens Advice Bureau?'

I felt panicky at her unease and said reassuringly: 'Yes, I'll talk to Simon and we'll get some advice', and our time was over.

As I drove home, my mind was jumping from thoughts about how to deal with our finances to feelings of confusion and rejection at Vida obviously not entering into any conversation about her personal life. That evening, and for the following weeks, Simon and I began to address our finances. Simon was very good at this and took advice then wrote letters to our credit cards explaining the situation. That was the beginning of having so little money that we could sometimes barely afford food but we managed to hang on to our home so the children were not too badly affected. Simon continued to apply for jobs, often getting interviews, and at the same time he had the occasional consultancy job. At the point of getting an interview for a job, much of my attention was taken with helping him and investigating the possible new location we might have been living in, yet Simon never received an offer of a job. I was heavily involved in my therapy and hardly noticed the time passing and the increasing number of unsuccessful job applications. I was back in another session of therapy in my childhood at fifteen years old.

'Julie is another friend who seemed to have no problem in finding pleasure in sex. The Christmas holidays have arrived and induce the usual panic in me that is relieved by Julie's visits. We happen to meet up with Mark and Russ and invite them to come over for an evening to play Ouija. We set it up and have drinks and while we are playing a message from the board reads that Julie should kiss Mark. We all giggle and she does. This carries on into a form of strip tease, the board telling us what clothes to remove. I do end up having sex with Russ, which I don't enjoy and makes me feel horrible, and, as he has not used a condom, I rush to the bathroom to try to "wash out" the sperm because I suddenly feel very scared of becoming pregnant.

'The new school term arrives and the teachers are talking about exam mocks, even for CSEs, and again I start the term with the intention of trying to do well and attend regularly and do my homework. A short while after this, I am running up to the biology labs and when I reach the top of the stairs I have a very strange bodily feeling. I am spinning around in my head, there is an odd heavy feeling in my pelvis, and have to press myself against the wall to stop myself from collapsing. I pass it off as "something weird" and don't tell anybody.

'Julie continues to come to my house each weekend and we often play Ouija until one evening we are playing and the letters spell out "y-o-u-a-r-e-w-i-t-h-c-h-i-l-d". We can't grasp what it is saying at first and ask it to spell it again: "M-a-r-i-a-n-i-s-w-i-t-h-c-h-i-l-d". Then whatever we ask, it keeps repeating that I am with child. We both laugh and think it ridiculous and we never play again. I do begin to think that something might be amiss with me and ask my mum if she thinks my "tummy is fat". She laughs at me saying: "Don't be ridiculous." I can't gauge from my periods whether I am pregnant because I am very irregular, so I reason that I am just having one of my longer times without a period and think that my "fat belly" is due to something like water retention.

'The February half-term is approaching and I have arranged to go to stay with Joss and Philippe (her boyfriend) who have a flat in a town near to Joss's university. Their flat is in the attic of a large Victorian terrace and has one big living room/bedroom so I am given a mattress on the floor at one end of the living room, and they sleep in a double bed at the other. Celine (our half-sister) is also going to come to stay for a couple of days. I'm beginning to have trouble closing my jeans (I'm usually very skinny) and quietly ask Joss if she thinks my belly looks a bit fat. She offers to have a look and as I stand sideways without my trousers on in front of her, her eyes nearly pop out of her head while she says, with a red face: "Could you be pregnant?"

I mumble: "Maybe."

She then tells me she'll talk to Philippe. I am beginning to feel very weird and floaty and events start to spin me into a vortex of numbness. Joss spoke to Philippe and, because he's a GP, they have decided that Philippe will give me an internal examination that evening to ascertain whether I am pregnant.'

I stopped talking and looked towards my therapist and she slowly said: 'It sounds like you had no say in what was happening to you.' I was feeling so embarrassed but managed to regain my flow.

'Joss tells me to remove my trousers and knickers and to lie on the table on my back with my knees up and legs apart and she stands behind me a couple of feet away, watching. Philippe then shines the desk light in between my legs and gives me an internal

33

with his bare fingers to feel if the womb is enlarged and he turns towards Joss. "It feels very large, like a grapefruit and it should be the size of a tomato." I am pregnant though all I feel is weird and floaty.

Vida suddenly burst in angrily: 'Why didn't they take you to a GP or give you a simple urine test?' I was taken aback by her question, particularly because she had never been angry like this before and I replied rapidly: 'I don't know', and continued.

'Joss decides that Celine should be told. She initially responds with silence but then the next day asks: "Does that mean I won't be able to go skiing at Easter because Dad has to pay for your abortion?" Joss and Philippe phoned my father who agreed to pay for a private abortion. I am taken to various doctors who again give me internals and say the same: that I'm pregnant by about eight to twelve weeks. The abortion is arranged (about ten days after finding out) and the situation gets even stranger.

'Philippe decides that because I am pregnant I should sleep with him and Joss in their bed and before we go to sleep he pats my belly saying: "Goodnight, baby." Meanwhile, Joss has sat me down and said to me: "Just think of it like a lump of shit that needs removing from your body." I only sleep in their bed for a couple of nights because it feels very creepy.

'The day of my abortion arrives and I'm taken to a beautiful looking house surrounded by wooded gardens. I am shown to a private room, am given a gown and then a nurse gives me a pre-med. Philippe is going to be in the operating theatre as an observer. Joss leaves and I am wheeled down to the theatre. Afterwards, I awake in my bed sobbing and screaming. The nurse comes in and tries to quieten me but I want my sister. I cry louder and louder occasionally shouting: "Joss, I want Joss!"

'The nurse returns and says to me very angrily: "You are upsetting the other patients. Be quiet." I fall back to sleep and when I awake Joss is there laughing because I made "such a fuss". I learn that Philippe fainted in the theatre and that they couldn't get the instruments into my cervix so they hadn't been able to do the abortion and they've arranged for me to come back next week for another one. Joss goes on and on about how it's because: "Your body isn't fully mature so your cervix is still small," so I have to wait another week for the pregnancy to end.

'On the morning of my second operation I awake early to hear Joss and Philippe having sex. I feel like dying with shame and humiliation. This reminds me of a time, about three years before, when I was staying with them both in Paris (I was thirteen years old). I was watching TV, while Joss is cooking and Philippe resting, when I start to hear strange noises. I go to investigate and am standing outside of Joss's and Philippe's bedroom and just as I'm about to knock to see what's wrong, I suddenly realise that they are having sex. I feel so embarrassed and return to watching the TV without saying anything because I just want to evaporate. Then it gets worse because, when Joss emerges from the bedroom and because I must have looked at her in an accusing or hurt way she looks at me defiantly saying: "It's none of your business" and swaggers away laughing.'

I shook my head, asking: 'Why did they have sex like that, so close to me, especially when I was due to have my abortion?' But I left no space for Vida to reply and rushed on.

'When I have my second operation they manage to "remove" my foetus and I bleed for days; I am no longer pregnant. I have to stay about ten days more for post-operative checks and, during this time, Joss speaks to me angrily and I burst into tears and run out of the flat. Philippe follows me but I can't share any of it with him and insist that he leaves me crying on my own in a park. I return and Joss says nothing. A few days later, I leave and my father picks me up from the train station. As we drive back to my mother's house he is prattling on about nothing and I turn to him and shout: "I've just had an abortion!" He replies: "Yes, and now it's finished." We never talk about it again. My mother doesn't say anything to me and everything returns to "normal".'

I had a few tears in my eyes and Vida gently passed me the tissues while whispering: 'Shall we continue next week?' I saw we had gone five minutes over our time.

Simon was very supportive towards my therapy and often sat listening to my summary of our sessions, making few comments (he actually thought my family were selfish bastards but didn't tell me that until some years later). The next session came and I somehow continued where I had left off (it was strange how, when deep into some issue, this happened effortlessly, as if the time apart had not existed).

'I return to school explaining that I was ill with flu, which nobody believes, as I have missed about a month of school. I have also missed all the mock exams and my history teacher gives me the mock during class time but I cannot concentrate and barely get any marks. After a couple of weeks of being home, I get ill with a very sore throat and swollen neck. I seem to lie there for so long alone but manage to get my mother to phone for the doctor. He comes and says I have a very bad throat infection and prescribes antibiotics (I now know that it was tonsillitis). My mother occasionally lurches into the room and roughly puts a tray of soup next to my bed; I feel very guilty for being ill and, as I lay in my room alone, I'm having strange daydreams of a woman telling me to "get in bed; get out, get in bed" repeatedly until I'm exhausted and I'm a very little girl in a nappy struggling to get off and on the bed.'

I turned to Vida (I often spoke to her with my head either bowed or slightly at an angle away from hers). 'This was when I started to have the images and feelings of terror about staying with that horrible woman when I was sixteen months old but I can't understand why I hadn't remembered it before this time.' My therapist looked directly at me, with a very serious face, making me feel scared.

'It was possibly because during your abortion you had been subjected to abusive situations that reminded you of the earlier abuse.'

I interrupted: 'What do you mean by 'abusive situations?'

'You know that the way that your sister and her boyfriend examined you could be viewed as a form of sexual abuse and, when they had sex with you in the room, that would definitely be considered abusive behaviour. Added to this, you had no control over the decision to have the abortion so the similarities between the situations were abuse and powerlessness.'

I said nothing for a while, staring fixedly at the tree just outside her window, and suddenly I began to speak again.

'A few months after my abortion, I still haven't had any periods and am worried something is wrong so, without telling anybody, I go alone to the doctor, who is an elderly man. I explain, in a halting slow voice, what the problem is and he asks me to undress completely and lie on his examination table. I lie there completely naked, not knowing why, and he stares at me, saying: "You have a fine body." He then tells me to lift my knees and open my legs and puts his bare fingers inside me and feels around, telling me that my cervix is badly scarred. At the same time he is stroking my right leg and gazing at me in a horrible way. He keeps "examining" me for ages asking me to do strange things like "cough" while staring at my breasts. I am so young and naïve that I have no idea what is happening; I can't believe a doctor would be doing something so awful as molesting me. I dress very shakily, as he watches me, and leave feeling very confused and upset. I don't tell anybody.'

'How could a doctor do that to me?' I shouted pleadingly at Vida.

She talked firmly and softly saying: 'The important thing is to know that he abused you and that he shouldn't have done it. It's the same thing with your sister and her doctor boyfriend, they shouldn't have examined you the way they did. The reason why these things happened to you is because you had no adult around to protect you. You were a vulnerable child.'

I fell into a stunned silence, I rarely cried because I automatically swallowed any sobs that might threaten to erupt. I drove home slowly, feeling overwhelmed with confusion and anger. I did sort of know that my relationship with Joss was not good, partly because she had a brittle, hard way of communicating, showing very few 'soft' feelings, and had often been nasty to me as a child and teenager. She had the knack of finding something about me that I was pleased with and taking great pleasure in spoiling it with ridicule (my mother never intervened) and over the years it did affect my fragile self-confidence (I'm still paranoid about being 'laughed at'). A typical comment from her was: 'You've done something different to your hair and it makes you look like a prostitute' (I was thirteen years old). I would not say anything back, my usual response being to sink into a morose silence, and there was nothing to ameliorate her onslaughts because I don't remember her ever giving me a compliment. I guess the truth (of which I had no idea) was that she really disliked me from the day I was born and that I was constantly trying to change her feelings for me by trying to please her. I now reciprocate her dislike but with some realisation that we are both victims of our shared childhood.

Chapter 4

I was in confused space, I didn't seem to be able to understand the point to life; I knew that I deeply loved my children and had to find some way to give them the security and education to enable them to have a 'normal' life, yet I was often in a deep suicidal depression. However, in my sessions with Vida I had hardly spoken about my daily problems in simply getting out of bed and managing to somehow get through another day. I was completely immersed in giving my therapist a detailed account of my early life and today I was trawling through my teenage years.

'It's my sixteenth birthday (a couple of months after my abortion) and, although I have no memories of a cake (I don't remember any birthday cakes in my childhood), I do remember being in a department store with my mother who is asking me to choose a new bike for myself. Some weeks earlier I mentioned to her: "It's not fair because Celine has a new bike; I've never had one." I have a Saturday routine of going out to town with my friend Julie and we have managed to get membership of a nightclub. I love the dancing and drink and dance until closing time at 1 a.m. I often get very drunk and begin to sob in some dark corner, occasionally telling some concerned person: "I've just had an abortion." At the end of the evenings, we walk through the town, stopping to buy chips or a hot dog, to the station and get a taxi back to my house and sleep until midday. On a couple of occasions, we meet a couple of blokes and invite them back to my house (my mother never seems to be aware of them in the house) but I don't have sex so they rapidly lose interest. I try to control my drinking because I am so embarrassed about having cried and told some person I don't know about my abortion. When sober, I sometimes allow myself to wonder what my baby would have been like; I imagine that she is a girl and that her spirit is close by, waiting to enter my next baby.

'After a few weeks, we begin meeting up regularly with a few blokes who are in their late teens and living in a shared house. They invite us back to their house after the club. They are heavily into pot, which we smoke with them all night while listening to great music that I haven't heard before. They are friendly and don't seem in a great hurry to get either of us into bed and I do like one of them a lot. Jack is tall and slim with dark hair and I think he is gorgeous. I think about him constantly and can't wait to get to the club each week to meet up with him.

'After a few weeks he comes back to my house alone with me. I am completely in love with him and feel wonderful when he holds me and strokes my hair, yet kissing is still a problem for me (it makes me feel sick) but because I adore him I carry on. We have sex without contraception but, despite me feeling wonderful when he hugs me, I feel nothing during sex except wanting it to be over. I continue to let him do it to me because I can't bear the thought of losing him. I spend nearly every minute of each day and night thinking about him and I start to have daydreams about having his baby and marrying him. I long for a baby; my arms ache to hold my baby.

'He doesn't ever take me out with him but often phones late on a Friday night after he's been to the pub and invites me to his flat. I always rush to him, riding on my bike late at night for about half an hour through dodgy back streets, heart pounding yet being so determined to be with him that I ignore my fears. I would arrive with bright, sparkly eyes and he would take me into his room, have some dope with me, then do it to me. I start to think I might be pregnant even to the point of "feeling" a baby move so I tell him that I think I might be having his baby. He looks very panicky, though he does buy a home pregnancy test and show me how me to do the test. But, to my great disappointment, it is negative. He only sees me occasionally after this but I still hang on to the possibility that he would realise how much he loved me and ask me to marry him.

'Meanwhile, I am supposed to be revising for my CSEs and O levels but I can't really see the point because I won't be able to get into a university to do a degree with CSEs. I can't think clearly about my future; I vaguely think a degree is a possibility because

Joss is doing one but I often find myself dreaming about having a baby.'

My brown-eyed, silently listening friend interjected: 'You were finding it hard to accept the loss of your pregnancy. It would have been different if you'd had someone like a counsellor to help you.'

I replied in a raised voice: 'I never had anybody to talk to until you.' Vida looked softly at me.

'Yes, I know.'

I continued.

'I don't know why I bother but I do go to school that summer to get my exam results, which is awkward because I have to ask what "U" means; the secretary looks embarrassed and says: "Unclassified". I have several U's, though I do get a B in O level French. I return home and mention to my mother my results to which she responds: "What are you going to do?"

'I reply: "I'd love to get married and have a baby."

'She stops cooking, stares at me in amazement and says absolutely nothing.

'Luckily, sometimes I meet up with a friend of my mother who has a four-month-old baby boy. I love to cuddle him and while with her talk about how: "I'd love to have my own baby." Her response is immediate.

'"You mustn't. You're far too young and you must get yourself a life. How would you look after it? Have you thought how boring it can be stuck in a house all day with no freedom and no money?" She goes on and on. "What about the baby's father? Don't they deserve a father that can care for them?" As I leave, she grabs my arm and pleads with me: "Don't do it. Wait until you're much older and can cope." I immediately go to the doctor and go on the pill. A lot of what she said had made sense and I now focus on getting to university.

'In the autumn, I return to school to go into the sixth form but feel awkward with all the "bright" young people who have stayed on; all my classmates left to get jobs. In the first few days, I happen to see a teacher from the previous year who says to me in a surprised and humorous tone: "What are you doing here?" After this, I can't return to the school but find out that I can take O and A levels at the local college of further education. I vaguely know that you need five O levels and two A levels to get into a university, so I decide to start by doing the O levels. I begin attending the classes and feel like I fit in because there is a very wide mix of students.'

My time had come and Vida was saying: 'You managed to hear a caring voice and began to change your life.' Then, after a silence, she used another variant of her closures: 'It's time to finish for this week' (I would never get used to the endings). Over the next few months I spent each therapy session telling and retelling her how I got a place at a poly to study for a degree.

'A few Saturdays into the autumn term I am at the disco with Julie and see Jack with another girl. I can't believe my eyes and, when he's at the bar, approach him to ask him if he'd like to dance. He refuses and is obviously embarrassed to see me. I have to face the truth and run from the club and walk the three miles home crying. I arrive home distraught, have some more booze then I find some tablets and sit in the toilet and take them. I go back into my room, lie in bed and begin to feel very scared of dying so I rush down to my mother's room, bursting through her door shouting: "I've taken some tablets," then run back up to my room.

'She does come up a few minutes later and asks: "What tablets have you taken?" I point to the brown bottle sitting on the corner of my chest of drawers. She walks over, picks it up, shakes it and looks in it. She then walks out without saying anything. I fall asleep and awake later to be violently sick on to the carpet. I go back to sleep, awake to the mess in the morning and, when I see my mother, she makes no reference to me possibly having tried to kill myself.'

I turned to Vida saying: 'I have never talked to my mother about this and sometimes wonder if she hoped I would die because how could she ignore what I had attempted to do? Why wasn't she concerned that I might do it again?'

Her brown eyes looked so sadly at me while she gently replied:

'Maybe your mother was so wrapped up in her own problems she didn't manage to see yours. What she did was dangerous. You could have died or been seriously ill through liver damage.' A long silence ensued with me staring at my favourite tree as the leaves swayed against Vida's window. My attention suddenly returned to my narrative.

'Towards the end of the autumn term I meet a girl in my English literature class who is looking for someone to share a flat with and I suddenly see how to escape from the house I hate and my confusing mother and immediately offer to move in with her. She has found a flat in a really nice area of the city and I can't wait to move. I think that I could pay for it in the same way that Jack has his flat; by claiming benefits. I go along to the benefit office explaining that my mother has thrown me out of her house so I have to live in a flat and they agree to pay the rent. We move in the middle of January and, when I know it is possible, I tell my mother.

'I am sitting in my mother's bedroom with my father (Mum was in bed) and say casually: "I'm thinking of moving into a flat with a friend."

'My mother's reaction surprised me because she looked shocked and said loudly: "What?"

'My father said laughingly: "Why not let her?"

'"Very well then," my mother said, in a dead tone.

'It is not discussed again and I soon begin to pack. My first memory of the flat is being in the kitchen with Jill preparing our evening meal together and she's explaining how sprouts need to be peeled. The kitchen is cold, damp and has an empty feeling and I am feeling strange and panicky. I just want to run away but I've got nowhere to go. The flat is in the attic of a very large Victorian house and is surrounded by mature trees and elegant avenues. Although I'm sharing the flat with Jill, she is often not around because she spends most of her time at her boyfriend's. The flat has no TV and the long evenings are particularly empty and I find it difficult to occupy myself. I use the time to begin reading my English literature books and eventually get into *Great Expectations*. The story distracts me from my problems and helps me to understand that life has been tough and lonely for others as well.

'I feel very alone some evenings but it is better being truly alone than alone at home with my mother so far away from me, yet in the next room. I think this helps me to realise that it is better for me to live away from my mother and I begin to settle into my new life. I meet Julie in town at the weekends and we go to the club and come back to my flat sometimes alone and, at others, with a circle of friends. I start to go out with Neil, a friend of Jack's. I don't particularly fancy him but I am his girlfriend for the next few years, until I go to poly. Neil and his family form an important part of my life. I have a routine with Neil: each weekend, we spend the Friday and Saturday out with friends then stay at my flat and on the Sunday we go to his parents' house for Sunday lunch. I love going to his house; the welcome on entering, the smell of the roasting lunch, the joy of all sitting together after lunch and watching a film on the TV. I leave late in the evening and return to my flat for the week of study at college. Neil has a job as a mechanic and is very tired in the evenings on the weekdays so we don't see each other. I accept that I have to have sex with him at least once during each weekend. I love his mother and spend all week looking forward to the Sunday.'

I remembered where I was and my attention shifted to Vida. 'I don't want to think what would have happened to me if I hadn't had her in my life at that time.'

Vida spoke gently to me. 'It sounds like she was able to care for you in a way that you hadn't often experienced.'

I responded enthusiastically: 'Yes, yes and I used to have long chats with her, though she often used to joke about how I was keeping Neil waiting and I should marry him.'

'At the end of the summer term, my flatmate tells me that the following year she's going to live with her boyfriend, so I decide to move back home for the summer and half-think that I might stay at home because I'm not sure about living in a flat on my own. In late July, I am booked into the hospital to have my wisdom teeth out. I am quite nervous and Neil takes me to my ward. I am admitted the evening before my operation into a small ward with one other girl my age. I awake after the operation with horrendous pain in my jaw, crying hysterically and telling the nurses to fuck off. They inject me with something and then I awake in the ward with a very swollen face and pain, such awful pain. The girl in the opposite bed has her parents with her and I have to wait until the evening for a visitor because Neil is working. Neil visits me that evening and looks very shocked at the size of my face. I am in hospital for four days and three nights and my mother and brother don't visit me once (my father is away in France).

'Neil takes me home on the fourth day, having taken the morning off work and, when I enter the house, my mother's reaction is to whoop and laugh at my swollen face and to say: "I must take a photograph." She rushes upstairs, gets her camera and then takes her time taking the photo by getting me to pose on a chair. I am in the most dreadful pain and am speechless at my mother's reaction. I retreat to my room for several days and have to phone Neil at his work to get me some more painkillers and some food, as there is nothing I can eat in the house. Ray shows no care and even shouts at me for being in the kitchen at the same time as him. I decide to find myself a flat for my last year at college.'

'Why was my mother (and the rest of my family) so oblivious to my pain? How would I have survived without Neil? I'm sure that without him I would simply have felt so shit that I might have committed suicide!' I left no space for any reply and rushed on.

'My bedsit is in a large Victorian terrace. My room is on the first floor and it's a lovely big room with an open bed area built half-way up the room, so that there is a ladder to get to the bed (like a bunk bed). Underneath the bed area is a small kitchen, which I really like as it's my own. The room has two very tall windows looking on to the mature tree-lined road and I love to see the trees and hear the birdsong. I still have to share a toilet and bathroom, which I really hate, but there are fewer people than my last flat so they are cleaner. I really like my new home and soon get into my routine of college in the week and Neil and his family at the weekends. Neil has a friend who has started to go out with a woman I really like and the Saturday evenings in the pub are often spent in a foursome.

'My father also visits me weekly to give me French lessons for my A level. The lessons with him are very useful for me because he teaches me techniques for learning that I use in my other subjects (I'd had no real order to my studying). The only problems I was having were recurrent nightmares of being chased by men and women who wanted to murder me; I would wake up sweating with terror, fumbling desperately for the light. Sometimes I was so scared I couldn't move towards the light switch and would huddle in a ball shape in my bed and remain as still as possible while in my head I would put all frightening images and thoughts into a hole in the ground, that was lined with concrete, and I would fall back to sleep while filling the hole with quick-setting concrete.'

I heard Vida asking: 'Do you still have nightmares?'

'I've had them since I was a small child and the first clear memory of one is when I'm about seven years old at my first boarding school. I awake in the middle of the night in terror and see a poster on the wall of a pop star and his eyes are so scary staring at me that I hide in a ball in my bed.'

I went on to ask: 'Do you think that dreams are important?'

'Yes, I think they can give us clues about what we might really feel and think about a situation,' Vida said with serious conviction. I jumped back to telling her about my life in my new flat.

'I remember my father bringing my mother to visit me and she's happily engrossed in talking when I mention that I need to leave as I've arrange to meet up with some friends. As soon as I have said that, she starts to groan loudly about her backache. I have never seen her so obviously reacting to a situation by using her back and, when alone with my father, ask him whether he noticed it also. He looks at me very sadly and says nothing.'

'You were beginning to understand something of your mother's illness,' Vida said in her gentlest voice. I swiftly moved on.

'Joss, Philippe and their toddler son Marc go to stay with my mother a few days before their flight to Australia because they were emigrating. I am really happy to see Marc again. I have loved him since seeing and holding him as a young baby. I have an argument with Joss over a shirt of mine. I sometimes take my washing to my mother's and am doing my ironing and as I am ironing my shirt Joss says: "That's a nice shirt. Why don't you give it to me?"'

'It's my favourite shirt so I take my courage and say with a reddened face: "No." To which she turns angrily to me, saying:

'"You're so greedy, aren't you?"'

'This is the last time I'm going see her before she leaves for her new life.'

I turned to Vida, speaking quickly and angrily: 'Why did she want my shirt? She was married to a well-paid GP, had a good degree (though she'd let me know that it would have been better if she hadn't had to deal with my pregnancy so close to her second year exams), a son and was about to go to live in a fabulous house in Australia. Why would she want my shirt when I had so little compared to her?'

Her brown eyes looked deeply into mine while she spoke. 'Relationships between siblings can become based very much in rivalry if envy is not managed well by parents.'

'Do you mean that the resentment she felt towards me around my birth has just carried on, maybe even getting worse, because my mother and father didn't notice and intervene?'

'Well, yes, that's probably what happened, though personality types also have an effect,' Vida stated in her very clear manner. I couldn't stop reviewing this time in my life.

'In the Easter holiday, after Joss has left, my father arranges for me to go on a French course that he is teaching to help me in my A level studies. His wife is also teaching and comes as well. The three of us arrive at the university halls where we will be staying and my father introduces me to a colleague of his as: "A friend of his daughter's". I feel very awkward and feel myself going very red.

'In the halls I make friends with one girl. I go to my meals with her and to the pub in the evenings. However, as the week progresses, having to pretend that I hardly know my father begins to take its toll, particularly as midweek it's my eighteenth birthday and he gives me an unsigned card with a few kisses and as I don't tell anybody else, there is no celebration. The lecture theatres are some way from the halls and my father gives a few of us lifts and, after one evening session with him doing the lecture, while in the car I just can't stop the tears rolling down my face. I try to hold it in and when we arrive I run to my room and then I go to phone my mother and tell her that I can't keep up the pretence. She says her usual empty, consoling words but contacts my father who comes to my room and tries to hug me saying: "All that matters is that I love you." I have no idea how to respond to him and say nothing.'

Vida rushed to speak, in a tense and furious way: 'Didn't they know anything about identity?' I looked at her very confused and simply jumped back in.

'I return to my flat feeling bruised and hopeless. This feeling persists after I go to visit my mother and she offers me a rug for my eighteenth birthday. My mother's way of getting presents is to order things she likes throughout the year from catalogues, then to search around in her piles of parcels for birthday and Christmas presents. However, Neil has given me a gold ring that he took me to a shop to buy and asked me to choose and I am very proud to wear it. His mother also took the trouble to find out which perfume I liked and bought me it; it feels so different being given a present specially chosen for me. I go out to celebrate my birthday with Neil and our friends and we return to my flat quite drunk. In bed, Neil is quite insistent about having sex and I get a bit scared, saying: "No, I don't want to" but he ignores me and carries on. I can't seem to get him to stop. The next day he apologises but I just feel numb. Soon after this, he moves to London and I am quite relieved to be away from him and I spend most of the weeks running up to my exams studying. I also apply to several universities to study biology and go to a couple of interviews.'

I looked to Vida and she said in her usual gentle tone: 'You found that your studies took you away from your problems?'

'Yes, that's right,' I replied before continuing.

'At the end of the exams I move back home as I'll only be there for a few weeks before I go to university. However, I'm desperately disappointed when the results come. I've only scraped through two A levels (I already had five O levels) which wasn't enough to get into university so I quickly find a place at a poly on an environmental science degree that will accept my low grades. Ray is living at home (he spends most of his time with his girlfriend, Jackie) and I'm getting on quite well with him and one day, as we meet in the kitchen, he casually says to me: "You know, Dad made a move on Jackie." I spin round.

'"What do you mean?"

'"You know, he asked to have sex with her." Ray repeats.

'I cannot believe that my dad could have done such a thing and feel any respect that I had left for him instantly evaporate. All I can say to Ray is: "That's awful and he's a fucking low bastard for doing that to you."

'I ask him if he's talked to Dad about it and he tells me: "No, but I've made Jackie promise to tell me if he tries it on again and if he does I'll flatten him."

'I spend the next few weeks packing my cases for poly and organising my grants and accommodation. I know that I will leave Neil when I meet someone else at poly but I say nothing and enjoy my last few weeks with his mother, having our warm conversations and her giving me her wonderful Sunday lunches. She does take me aside one day and look seriously at me saying: "You're leaving him. Will you ever marry him?" I look back at her, saying nothing, but have tears welling in my eyes because I don't want to leave her. A few days later, Neil drives me to my poly accommodation.'

'You had worked very hard to get the chance to study for a degree and it shows how strong you are.'

Vida made this comment with such seriousness that I was embarrassed and mumbled: 'See you next week.'

Chapter 5

It was hard to believe that nearly three years had passed since starting therapy. Much of my time with Vida was spent going over and over what had happened to me. I couldn't seem to make sense of my childhood because in my mind it was like a chaotic muddle of random events. It's surprising how repetitive it can get but somehow, each time an event is retold, the reality becomes clearer and new, previously unknown, significant details can be uncovered. I think that what confused me most about my family is that they were thought of, by themselves and outsiders, as decent people. My father was convinced he was God's gift to women and academia and walked with his chest constantly puffed out. My mother saw herself as a very kind and generous person and refused to acknowledge her less appealing aspects. If any discussion began about her negligent care of me she dismissively ascribes it to her 'bad luck' at having always had back problems that the 'stupid doctors couldn't make better'. It wasn't until this time in my therapy that I started to seriously question my mother's version of events.

My weekly session had come around and I was, as usual, following Vida's petite frame down the dark corridor and longed to touch her warm body. We entered into her sanctuary, which smelled of her soft, gentle perfume, and she sat deliberately in her chair. I usually had to push mine slightly back from hers before I could sit awkwardly down. The beginning had become a tense moment. I looked shyly towards Vida and she looked directly at me. I tentatively asked her: 'Are you interested in my dreams?'

She looked animated and nodded emphatically. 'Yes, yes of course.'

I told her of a recent dream that kept coming into my head and as I told Vida this dream my breathing became fast and panicky and I felt dizzy and sick.

'I'm at a very crowded swimming pool and there are two older women trying to drown me. One of them has hold of my head under the water and I'm struggling like mad to get free. I manage to break free and am trying to run through the water (we were in the shallow end) away from them but they're gaining on me. I wake up, sweating with terror, not knowing whether they catch me.'

The room was silent, my breathing noisy (I was trying to control it while hoping that Vida hadn't noticed) and my brown-eyed friend looked more alert than she had for a while. She shifted in her chair, took a slow breath, and tentatively said: 'That's a very interesting dream and I wonder if that's how you experienced your mother and sister when you were a child.'

I felt quite uncomfortable because I could sort of see Joss being like that but had clung on to the belief that my mother did, underneath, want the best for me. It did get me thinking and I began to remember my mother saying to me that I reminded her of her younger sister. I had often heard her comment, in a tired exasperated way: 'Yes, being so highly strung you were both difficult children.' She had disliked her younger sister when they children and they only exchanged Christmas cards as adults.

I turned to Vida, asking: 'Do you think that because I remind my mum of her younger sister she sort of treats me like her?'

'Well, yes, that can be how patterns of relationships continue along family lines, particularly if there are many unresolved painful childhood issues in the relationships.'

I left the session thinking about my mother's relationships. It occurred to me that the only person she had consistently seen was her older sister. She did have a younger brother with whom she didn't exchange Christmas cards; could this explain her detachment from my brother? She often said that as a baby he didn't like to be cuddled. She didn't have any long-term friends and had spent most of the years since I went to poly living with my sister. Was her relationship to Joss similar to that she had with her older sister? This set the trend for the next months of my therapy; I was trying to understand my relationship to my mother and revisited many childhood memories.

'As a very young child I often have tonsillitis and my mother's reaction is to pull a disgusted face with a retching noise while saying: "Oh your breath is terrible." I have my tonsils out at two and a half and the doctors and nurses are discussing whether to put me in a cot or a bed. They decide to put me in this horrible cot with huge, thick, black iron bars. My mother comes to visit me and, as she leaves I become, hysterical and am standing at a window watching her leave, banging repeatedly on the glass. The nurses carry me back to my "cot".

'During the summer that I was three years old I get a badly infected toenail and the doctor decides it needs removing. Mum takes me to the nurse, who marches me into a room with a scalding bath of water. She plunges my toe in (I scream in agony) and then uses a pliers-type instrument to rip my toenail out. The pain is unbelievable, worse because the nurse seems to enjoy it, and she tells me to stop being a baby. I come out of the room, and my mother has a toy cart for me to ride on, and she insists that I sit on the cart and ride around in the yard outside the health centre.'

I stopped, looked at Vida, feeling confused and angry, and she took her cue.

'It seems to me that your mother wasn't able to be with you emotionally.'

I was still feeling confused and asked: 'Do you mean that she couldn't hold my pain inside her and so had to push it away?'

'Yes, yes empathising with someone else is the capacity to feel their pain and to want to help ease their suffering.'

After one of my long staring silences I changed my narrative to happier times.

'My mother has inherited some money from her gran so we move to a glorious large Victorian redbrick semi. I love the house; it has a grand front door with lovely sparkly coloured glass, a large hall, three big reception rooms, big kitchen, a downstairs bathroom and a conservatory. The upstairs has four bedrooms and Ray and I share the large front bedroom with a huge, graceful bay window that is like a glorious suspended mid-air den.

'The best of all is the endless back garden, which has a square lawned area with colourful borders then, even better, an orchard with two rows of ten apple trees either side of a path and at the bottom are the hens. My mother makes the house beautiful, particularly because she has inherited wonderful antique furniture from her gran. In the hall she places an old grandfather clock that makes us all safe by looking stern. The front drawing room is all perfect and straight, just for grown-ups. My mother one day allows me into the grown-ups room to show me her new gramophone, a large oval wooden piece of furniture that looks like a sideboard but has sliding doors on the top which open up to reveal a record player and a radio. She puts a record on and we dance and sing which I love. Then she says: "You mustn't tell Daddy about it," which really confuses me because it is so wonderful. I play upstairs and in the garden for what seemed like an infinite amount of time, and mostly I play with Ray and local friends (my sister was often with her own friends). My mother cooks pillow-like fluffy cheese soufflé (my favourite) and the four of us sit happily around the kitchen table.'

I sighed heavily. 'I feel such a longing telling you this; if only my mother had managed to keep it going, but I suspect that this was partly to try to entice my father to leave his wife.'

'You had a happy time in your life and it's very disappointing that it couldn't last', Vida said. I picked up my thread.

'Mum then meets a man through work, Robert, and starts to see him and apparently my dad takes him out for a drink and persuades him to marry my mother and to legally declare that he is our real father. My mother was "slightly annoyed" by what my father did but I guess she is desperate for some support so goes along with it and the planning goes ahead for them to marry in the July of my fourth year. However, my father has to have a "goodbye fuck" and my mother becomes pregnant, secretly hoping, I feel, that at last my father would see her and marry her, which doesn't happen so she has an abortion just before she gets married. While my mother has the abortion I am cared for by a very kind teacher. Ray goes somewhere else, as does Joss. My mum seems to have absolutely no qualms about splitting us up, sending us anywhere someone would have us and she often tells me, in an indignant, self-righteous tone, of how she even rings the Social Services in desperation but they turn her down so she pleads with a teacher who agrees to take me. She is a lovely, warm woman and I want to stay with her for ever and, I suppose, she feels like a fairy godmother. I begin to dream of living in another world, the world of fairytales and magic.

'Ray and I aren't invited to the wedding and are sent to stay with Mrs Jones. Joss is allowed to go as she is considered old enough. All I remember of this time is one evening. I am having boiled eggs for tea (we often do as it is mum's "fall-back tea") and I want two. Robert says that I'll be sick if I have two but mum gives them to me. That night I awake and am sick on the landing outside my mother's and Robert's bedroom. He rushes out and slaps me hard in the face, saying: "It serves you right." My mother then comes out and tells him to go back to bed.

'My next very clear memory (like a full-colour film in my head) is coming down to the kitchen and seeing my mother sitting at the kitchen table, her head in her arms, crying. I sit and put my arm around her, Ray does the same on the other side of her, and I try to tell her it'll be all right, feeling desperately helpless. I don't really know what happened but, after only two weeks of marriage, he leaves in the middle of the night (a few days after his mother had met my mother for the first time). Joss is not at home because she is away for nearly the whole summer in France, staying with a lover of my father. It is around this time that, according to Celine (my father's legitimate daughter), her mother cries for weeks on end and does not tell her why. Later, her mother tells her that her (my) father had told her about his illegitimate family but that his affair with my mother had ended because she had married another man. Celine's mother doesn't leave my father and their marriage remained "intact" until he dies twenty-five years later.'

'If only my dad had come to live with us; we needed him more', I said imploringly to Vida.

'It's difficult for you to see how your father could ignore your mother's, yours and your sister's and brother's need of him?'

'I hate my father for what he did to us.'

It was that time again and I walked from Vida's room feeling like my body was filled with lead.

I arrived back home, it was nearly Christmas, and I sat with Simon to discuss what presents we were going to give the children. He looked at me awkwardly. 'I've got some bad news to tell you: we've got no money left in the bank.' I suddenly felt myself sliding into a huge hole of swirling panic. I couldn't think of not being able to give my children Christmas presents. They were both deprived (new clothes and toys and holidays) compared to their friends (we lived in a village that was largely made up of middle-class professionals), which was affecting their friendships, schoolwork and general self-confidence (though, at the time, I wasn't fully aware of this). I was frantic for days wondering how I could find some money for presents. I considered trying to get a job but I was often ill with flu-like symptoms that would come on randomly, lasting for days. I had stopped believing that the doctor could cure me and, as long as I could manage to look after the children, I tried to carry on my daily routine. After a few days, I chose my only option and I phoned my mother, briefly explained my problem, and she surprised me by immediately offering to send me some cash. My relief was tremendous and I did feel very grateful to my mother. I still didn't understand why Simon was seemingly incapable of having consistent work (especially having his degrees and post-graduate experience) and kept encouraging him in his job applications and in his attempt to start his own consultancy. I had spent a few sessions with Vida talking about Simon's work problems and she also seemed to believe that he would soon get something solid. I was also trying to address my own job problems as the previous autumn I had enrolled on a diploma in counselling with a long-term view to developing a career as a counsellor, though my tiredness sometimes meant that getting to the weekly lectures was like walking through treacle.

The Christmas holidays were over, which was always such a relief to me. Around Christmas I most often (since I was a small child) find myself moving between feelings of desperate panic and excited anticipation. I sometimes wondered whether this was something to do with the fact that I never had a Christmas with my father and I did think it odd that I had not one memory of a

Christmas dinner. The theme of Christmas was the focus of my session with Vida immediately after our three-week break.

'The Christmas that holds the strongest memories for me is when I am about five years old and I am lying in bed (we have bunk beds and I am on the top). My mother is leaning over me saying: 'Remember that a man comes to see me to ask if the children are asleep and, if you aren't, he will take you all away.' This makes me so scared I will myself to sleep. I wake up later and can't feel the stocking in its usual place at the foot of my bed so I reason that, as I had already been asleep, the man must have come and gone and I go to investigate. As I walk towards the living room, I see my mother and sister filling the stockings. I am devastated and say dramatically: 'You've lied to me all these years. How could you?"

'My mother laughs loudly and tells me not to be silly.

'The next day my dream present has arrived; a Tiny Tears doll. I adore her (though for some reason I have no name for her) and I decide she has too much hair for a baby so I cut most of it off and feel disappointed that she still doesn't look like a real baby. Despite her strange hair, she's my baby and I love her totally and feed her and change her wet nappy (even though you have to squeeze her tummy quite hard to get her to wee). My favourite game is mummies and daddies (I play this up until I'm about eleven years old), which I play constantly with the boys from next door and my brother, although Ray often gets fed up with it and wanders off. We make a den and I and the older boy are the mummy and daddy. I somehow know that I should lie down and pull my pants down and I tell him to lie on top of me, and then we lie there, face to face, awkwardly staring at each other.'

I looked towards Vida. 'What's so strange about this memory is that I can clearly remember feeling confused because I am hating what we are doing yet I instigated it.' I immediately turned to staring fixedly at the bare tree brushing across Vida's window. Vida then shifted in her chair, took a slow breath and spoke.

'You were playing a normal childhood game yet you found it distressing.'

I made no comment and my account moved to starting school.

'I start school in that year and love it. I have a long line of gold stars next to my name (even though we still have Robert's last name, which I hate) and the teacher is soft, warm and kind. I have friends and love play times. I really enjoy the games with skipping ropes where two girls hold a rope at each end and, as they spin the rope, we run in and out, seeing if we can manage to run in, skip twenty times, and run out again without tripping. I hate the stinking cold toilets and avoid going. I mostly like the food. Our classroom has windows down to the floor on one side, so it's bright and sunny. We also have a pet rabbit, who I love to stroke. I feel so safe and warm in the classroom.

'I adore singing in the assemblies; my favourite song is "All things bright and beautiful", which I sing as loudly as possible. I feel exuberant and so happy when at school and miss it at the weekends. The weekends at home can be very lonely, as we hardly see my father and my mother has few friends and family that visit. At home, I often have loud frenzied tantrums, lying on the floor kicking and screaming. My mother's stock response is to say: "Where has my nice little girl gone?" If I try to tell my mother about Joss and Ray being nasty to me her repetitive answer is: "Don't tell tales"; she has a rigid policy of never intervening.

'I sometimes walk to school with Joss (when she hasn't run off with her friends) and have one vivid memory of her saying to me that she would marry a lawyer or a doctor with curly hair. I look at her feeling that somehow no one would want to marry me and I'm so confused as to why I can't be like her.

'The summer holidays come around and my father thinks my mother needs a rest so sends her to the south of France for a month with me only. My brother is sent to another foster home and my sister goes to her first holiday camp (*colony de vacances*) for children in France (she continues to go each summer until she is about fourteen and Ray and I join her when I am about eight years old). While on holiday alone with my mother, I miss my brother so much and am lonely and bored. We go to the beach each morning; I try to play in the sea alone while my mother sunbathes. In the evenings we go for walks along a tree-lined avenue with lots of elderly women sitting and men playing boules. They come up to us to stroke and touch my blonde-white hair and say how pretty I am which I hate. I just can't bear the attention.

'On the way home, we stay in Paris with a French friend of my mother and, as we are leaving, I realise I have left Tiny Tears in the flat, which is up several flights of stairs. I cry and plead with my mother to go to get her but she insists we haven't got time and that her friend will send her back home to us. I give up and feel bereft for the whole journey home and wait anxiously for her return. She arrives in a box that terrifies me, as she might be suffocated, but she's intact and I'm so happy to be reunited with my Tiny Tears.

'I am soon back at school (thankfully) and continue to enjoy the whole sequence from getting up in the morning and dressing (myself) and then entering a magical world of education and play. I just can't understand those who don't like school. I work very hard at my handwriting and get so frustrated that it is never as neat and tidy as I want it. Maths is a particular joy because of the neatness of placing the numbers on the squared paper and because they don't confuse me. I see numbers so clearly. I never talk about my mummy and daddy and concentrate hard on being at school and nowhere else.

'I am finally invited to a party, which thrills me. I love the idea (I hadn't been to any) and the pretty dresses. I have a velvet dress, which feels sublimely soft, and have a bow at my chest. My mother drives me to the party and, as she is giving another woman a lift, I am in the back and I must catch the door handle because I fall out of the back door. I manage to somehow grab on to the front seat belt and the door with my legs still in the car. My mother is talking and talking to this woman, while still driving, with me hanging out of the car door nearly falling out at the bends in the road. I am so terrified I can't speak; no words will come out to tell her. She finally sees me and brings the car to an abrupt halt but my party dress is ruined so I won't go to the party.

'My sixth birthday comes and I am given a high chair and pram for Tiny Tears, which is fantastic. My mother has also managed to organise a party for me. I am so excited and can't wait. The party is going well with lots of children when I notice Mum has disappeared. I find her in the bathroom with the boy next door who has raging diarrhoea that seems to be everywhere and absolutely stinks. The sickening smell fills the room with the party food (the downstairs bathroom is next to the kitchen) and, instead of sending him home, my mother puts him in the bath and cleans him and the bathroom up. The party is ruined and this is the only birthday party I ever have.'

'It's as if things in my life would seem OK but then be completely fucked up by some sort of mad chaotic event.' I was speaking in a defeated hopeless tone.

'Yes, it does seem that your mother had a need to ignore your feelings', Vida replied in her gentlest voice. My thoughts were still with birthdays.

'My seventh birthday is also a disaster. I don't remember anything except being so angry that I steal money out of my mother's purse – a note – which I don't think I had done before, and go to the local wool shop to buy myself a birthday present, which is a pink case with a dolly hair brush set that I want for my Tiny Tears. I am playing with it in my bedroom and my mother notices it and asks where I got it from. I blush terribly and blurt out what I have done. She is furious and tells me to put it back how it was and, literally, drags me by the hand to the shop. We enter, there are other customers in the shop chatting, and my mother barges through, shouting loudly.

'"My daughter has stolen money from me to buy this case and I want a refund and you are NEVER to serve my daughter again."

'The shop becomes silent and all eyes are on me, the shame and humiliation are unbearable. I twist free of my mother's hand and race back home. I fling myself on my bed and cry for hours.'

I turned towards my brown-eyed friend with a desperate feeling of confusion.

'My mother never mentioned it again and I felt so ashamed and bad.' Vida looked directly into my eyes while speaking firmly.

'Again, your mother lost an opportunity to understand why you might do something like that. Perhaps you were trying to tell her about your needs in the only way you knew how, being such a young child.'

I sought refuge in gazing towards the sad, bare branches of my tree and, in my usual way, my thoughts moved on.

'That autumn, Joss goes to boarding school, apparently at her request, although my mother says that she was becoming a difficult teenager so it was better she went. The house feels too empty, as if I had found her distant presence comforting. However, it was at this time that I have my first clear memories of my father because he often comes in the early evenings to take me and my brother for a drive around the town. He likes taking us to see the huge condensing towers of the gas works. He always says how marvellous they are but I just think they are huge, scary, and stinky. Then he sometimes takes us through the car wash, which has my brother and I in fits of giggles and he laughs with us. He also picks us up from school some days, which always makes me feel so special.

'During this time, on my way home from the sweet shop, a man tries to lure me into his car by offering me sweets and a lift home. I say no and feel my heart pounding and, shaking all over, I race home to tell my mother who asks me if I'm sure, but does absolutely nothing.'

'This reminded me that my mother mentioned to me some years ago that while Mrs Jones was looking after Ray she got a letter saying that the woman was "sticking pins" in her son. She said to me: "What was I supposed to do?" She did nothing.'

'Why does she never fight for us? I just can't understand her lack of protective instinct around us', I said forlornly.

Vida was shifting in her chair and said rapidly: 'Your mother was not able to take seriously threats to her children, which was inexcusably neglectful, and must have caused you both considerable pain.' After a deep silence Vida glanced gently at the watch on her wrist. 'We'll continue next week, shall we?'

On my drive home I thought about my mother, she confused me and I couldn't figure out what her genuine feelings were (and are) for me. I knew that whenever I was with her, I felt an awareness of a horrible knot in my stomach (even when talking with her on the phone) and she made comments that sent me demented with anger. Occasionally my anger towards her burst out and then she asked, in a superior, patronising, slow tone: 'What's wrong with you, Marian?' which sent me even madder and I either snapped back, 'nothing', or removed myself from her vicinity by either walking out on her or slamming down the phone. She never followed up an incident like that; the next time we had contact she acted as if nothing had happened.

My next session arrived and I was desperate to tell Vida of a dream I had after our last meeting.

'I'm in one of our therapy sessions. The room is slightly different because it looks a bit like my mum's guest living room in the house I loved. An old radio (like my mother's) has a Radio 4 programme on and a man with a very deep voice is saying: "Marian's illness is dementia praecox."'

'What does dementia praecox mean?' I asked Vida. She smiled broadly, almost laughing.

'It's an old psychiatric term for schizophrenia and I don't think you have that at all.'

I sat in silence, not really understanding why I would have such a dream and feeling confused at Vida's reaction but I said nothing and broke the silence by continuing with my early childhood.

'I'm in my seventh year, and my mother has decided that the only solution to her dilemmas around our care is to send us to boarding school and we spend the next few months being taken around possible schools that fill me with foreboding. The one place I love is my school and she's taking me away with my brother because she can't manage to look after us.

'"Let's face it, darling. It is better to go to boarding school than to go to foster homes," she often tells me, so I should feel "lucky" that she cared enough to send us to boarding school.

'She seems to ignore, or is unaware of, how much I enjoy school and how clever I am and chooses Summerhill, a "free" school, where children are "free" to decide whether or not they attend lessons. My father was, according to my mother, distraught, because education means everything to him (it's how he escaped his working-class background) but he isn't upset enough to do anything that changes the situation.'

I sat silently, slumped in my chair. Vida spoke gently to me.

'You were very happy at your first school yet your parents were sending you away.' I shifted to remembering my first days at boarding school.

'I am seven and a half years old standing on a train feeling like my world has ended. I am immobile and stiff; my face is fixed in a rigid mask staring out of the window. I want to sob hysterically and beg Mummy to take me home but I know it would be useless. My mother is on the other side of the window making "funny" faces at me, sticking her tongue out and putting her hands at her ears and wiggling them. She is trying to make me laugh and I am dying with fear and loss. I am being sent away from everything that I have grown to love: my home, my school, my friends and my father. The train carriage is full of "Summerhillian" children and is very noisy and chaotic. Ray and I remain seated in the same place and hardly talk to anyone.

'We arrive and all file on to an old bus. I feel suffocated with a desperate hopelessness yet I have no idea what is awaiting us at the "free school". I have no memories of actually arriving but after a while I begin to realise it isn't so bad, particularly because I do enjoy getting regular meals that were not boiled eggs and because I really like our live-in teacher; she is young, warm and very gentle from somewhere like Sweden. I try to go to some lessons but they're not like my old school; we seem to sit there for an age while the teacher finds us something to do, because they seem surprised that I and my brother have turned up (I have taken him along with me because my father had told me to teach my brother to write).

'I soon give up going to the unwelcoming lessons and the days then become an ocean of extreme boredom, with absolutely nothing organised for us to do all day and every day, so we hang around in the small woods or, if it's raining, in the hall. I send a letter each to my mother and father (I still have them as my mother keeps all letters sent to her). The letter to my mother thanks her for choosing this school because I like it and expresses hope that she is well; the letter to my father tells him that I've tried to teach Ray to write but I can't. My mother took the opportunity of our move to change our last name back to her maiden name (although Robert's last name was still on our birth certificates) so we readjust to our original name, which never had any connection to our dad. I miss my dad a lot during these first few weeks as I have been used to seeing him nearly every day during term times. In fact for the next few years, we hardly see him because our school is several hours drive from his home.'

I stopped and stared at my favourite tree. A tear tried to roll down my face and Vida offered me the box of tissues. I began to speak: 'The boredom was terrible. I had loved lessons at my old school.' Silence engulfed the room again. Vida uncrossed her legs, adjusted her jumper and looked at me.

'This was a terrible blow for you to lose your sanctuary of learning and your outings with your father.'

I cut in angrily: 'I hate my mother and my father for what they did to me.'

'You are very angry with your parents for not being able to care for you as you needed them to?'

'I loathe them both. How can they say that they loved us?'

'You cannot understand how they could have sent you away and you feel very angry with them?'

I gave up and retreated into a dead silence until the end of the session.

That week I dreamt that I was driving to my session and I saw Vida passing me in a car going in the opposite direction. I was quite confused about this dream until, a day before my seeing her, a phone call from her secretary cancelled our next meeting because she was ill. As usual, I spent my next days eagerly looking for the post, but nothing arrived. I phoned her secretary, who told me: 'Vida has a chest infection and it may be a couple of weeks before she's back.'

I was in turmoil, and had flashes of daydreams of the secretary phoning me to say that Vida had died. I couldn't imagine how I would live without her. Finally, another phone call let me know that she'd see me the next day (not our usual day). I entered her room in a tense agitated way and threw myself on to my chair. Vida smiled.

'I'm sorry that I've been ill.'

I asked aggressively: 'Are you better?'

'Yes, yes I am', Vida replied with a broad smile.

'You don't look it.'

Vida went bright red and sat looking angrily at me. I felt terrible and confused as to why I would be like that with her. After a very long silence, I started, tensely.

'I hate sitting in the waiting room for you before my sessions. The other patients sometimes scare me and I hate being looked at by all the people who work here and I particularly hate it when you're late.' Vida shifted in her chair and leant slightly forward.

'Well, you could come up to my corridor and sit at the end if that would be easier for you.'

'I'll try it next time', I said sullenly. Another long gap of empty silence ensued then I was speaking again and the words came before I knew what I was going to say. 'How much longer do you think I'll need to see you?'

Vida looked surprised and took some time to answer.

'Well, I have thought about it and I was thinking that maybe we could discuss the possibility of working towards an ending sometime during the summer. Of course, this is something that we can discuss further when you feel you need to and it's not set in stone. We can discuss this until you feel comfortable with the date of our last session. Endings can be difficult and they often need planning carefully but it is something that we decide together. Everybody is different and that's why there is no set way in which an ending happens. Of course, we can discuss this as much as you want.'

She just seemed to go on and on talking while I felt like I was falling further and further into a huge dark hole. I finally responded to her in a completely dead voice, my lips hardly moving, my face a rigid mask. 'I'll think about it.' I said nothing for the rest of the session.

I arrived home and felt numb for many days to come. I was like a robot yet I did manage to keep up the daily tasks of looking after my children (I was short-tempered with them) and I had bad arguments with Simon. My state of mind wasn't helped by another call from Vida's secretary cancelling our next two sessions because Vida was ill again. My mind was a jumble of her last words to me and it is as if all I could hear was 'ENDING' being shouted and replayed repeatedly in my head for many days.

After a while, I began to hear her other words more clearly, particularly her assurances that it was something that 'we discuss together, until you feel comfortable. We can discuss it as much as you want.' I came out of my automated state with the thought that I would discuss this further with my brown-eyed friend.

I drove nervously to my next session, going over and over what I might say. I couldn't stop my thoughts repeating themselves in a seemingly endless spiral of versions of what I might say to Vida (this has been going on for days). I sat in my new safe seat waiting for her and I felt special, having a seating area to myself. She opened her door and beckoned me to her and as I walked towards her door I could hardly breathe and felt dizzy. I sat breathlessly down and she again said: 'I'm sorry I've been unwell.'

Before I could stop myself I burst out loudly: 'Are you chronically sick or something?'

Her eyes widened and she fired back in a stern tone: 'I don't plan on being sick, you know.'

I sat feeling aghast at what had just happened and wished desperately that I wasn't with her. After a while, I tried to smile with my most bright, likable face.

'I'm sorry. I shouldn't have spoken to you like that.'

Vida smiled towards me.

'Thank you.'

I couldn't believe what I then asked.

'Were you angry with me?'

She smiled even more.

'No, not at all.'

I sat, so confused and said: 'Were you definitely not angry with me?'

'No,' she repeated. 'Why would you think I was angry with you?'

I gave up and looked longingly at the bursting buds on the branches of my tree that was motionless outside the window that day. My thoughts turned to my prepared 'speech' about our ending and I timidly began.

'I didn't like what you said to me about the timing of our ending.'

Vida gently replied: 'What didn't you like about what I said?'

A long silence followed, with me staring fixedly at a picture on her wall. 'Did you choose that picture?'

'Yes, yes I did.'

It was a framed poster of a busy library, the centre being a table of seated people reading and writing, with some getting up to leave and some getting ready to sit, all holding books. It was another of my favourite staring places. I managed to return to my original thread.

'I didn't want you to suggest an ending time. I wanted you to tell me that it would never end.' I flushed red with embarrassment. Vida looked at me softly.

'I'm very glad that you told me this. It's important for me to hear how you feel.'

I was stunned, and walked from the session elated.

Chapter 6

Vida's bout of illness was over and I settled into the next months of sessions by continuing to tell her of my experiences at boarding school.

'I have brought my Tiny Tears to Summerhill with me. She lies tucked up safely, hidden in my bed, during the day, as no one else has a dolly, but I do try to sneak to see her just to make sure she's all right, and at night we cuddle close. Then, a couple of weeks after starting, I see a crowd of slightly older children surrounding something burning and looking towards me laughing. They hold it up on a stick. It's Tiny Tears. They're burning my Tiny Tears. There's too many of them for me to do anything and it's too late, as Tiny Tears is already black and flaming. I can't watch any more and run to my bed and cry and sob, so desperately wanting her back. No adult notices, not even my special Swedish lady and I am devastated and wish I didn't exist. I tell nobody and miss her desperately, particularly at night, and I can't get the picture of the group laughing at her melted corpse out of my head.'

'Why would they do that to me and why didn't anybody notice?' I said while looking towards Vida with a deep feeling of hopelessness.

'You had nobody to comfort you in your terrible loss,' Vida said with watery eyes. I sat in a dark silence as time ticked slowly by and I moved on.

'Once the intensity of the "death" of Tiny Tears passes the days begin to blur into one long space of deep boredom, occasionally it lifts when I go to basket weaving classes in the woodwork building or to Ulla's room to weave on her loom. The loom fascinates me. How can all the horizontal and vertical threads be magically transformed into a whole piece of solid material? I spend as much time as possible with her as she patiently teaches me to weave and knit. Sometimes, other staff members are in her room, particularly Rob who lets me sit on his knee and touch his face. I love his craggy, floppy skin around his cheeks and always want to touch him. He was very tolerant!

However, there is so much time when no adults seem to be anywhere and a crowd of us, which includes my brother, hang around really bored and sometimes have "adventures" around the local railways (which involves running over train tracks) and in the local farms.

One day, we're just wandering around bored outside our dorm building and find a used condom. Somehow we all know what it is and we know that the Swedish lady has had to have an abortion. I don't know who thought of it but one of us knocks at her door and asks her to come outside to show her something. She comes out, smiling kindly at us. Chris then holds up the used condom by a stick and shouts: "You should have used one of these." We all join in and begin chanting and laughing: "You should have used one of these." She puts her hand up to her mouth and a huge sob comes out and she runs back to her room. We never see her again and I feel so guilty and sad and miss her terribly.'

'I still feel the confusion of why I was so nasty to someone who I really like,' I murmured.

'Maybe you were disappointed in her for not noticing that Tiny Tears had disappeared so she had become yet another adult who had not managed to see your needs.' I stared at the newly emerging leaves on the gently swaying branches of my beloved tree. Suddenly I was speaking again.

'On an escapade to a local farm, we see a big metal container of pig shit. We have to go up a ladder to look into the tank and someone dares me to swim in it. They start to goad me and say I'm a chicken and that I am too scared to swim in the shit. I have absolutely no idea why but suddenly I become furious and climb in and start to swim across the tank. In the meantime, the farmer has come out and begins to shout at us. He then sees me halfway across the tank and becomes speechless then he gathers himself and yells at me to get out. I frantically swim back to the ladder, jump out and we all run like mad.'

I looked towards Vida. 'I have no memory of how I got cleaned up but I do remember the look of utter confusion on the farmer's face, mixed with sadness for me and the other children were also very quiet with me, looking at me with a mixture of shock and sympathy.'

My brown-eyed friend gave me another clue to myself.

'Maybe you were expressing something of how you felt about your life?' I ignored the implications of what she had said and ploughed on.

'We smoke regularly and are always on the scrounge for fags. We even go looking for tabs on the ground that are long enough to smoke. The next holiday I remember is the summer when we're back home in the house I love, but Mum is packing all our things up as she has a job close to Summerhill and we are moving. She has sold all the toys I had for Tiny Tears; I protest half-heartedly and she responds by commenting: "You've grown out of all that, haven't you?" I was eight years old. I see my old primary school friends but they fall away as soon as their parents hear my new range of vocabulary; I have learned at Summerhill that swear words are to be spoken nearly every other word and the word "fuck" was a particular favourite of mine.

'My father tries to save our education by sending us back to our local primary school for the last two weeks of term (boarding school terms were a couple of weeks shorter than day schools), which is awful because I now can't do any of the maths and my handwriting is still so messy. It's so humiliating and I spend my time trying to hide my ignorance. In one lesson, I surreptitiously try to copy a sum off a boy but he notices and puts his hand up to tell the teacher in front of the whole class. I can't understand why I am so bad at school now (the teacher obviously hadn't been told that I had been at a "free" school for the last school year) so I'm now considered "thick", whereas the previous year I was "exceptionally bright".

'My dad drives us to and from the school and one day I keep switching the radio channels and he slaps me hard around the face for not stopping, I can still feel my face glowing red with pain and humiliation.

'During the rest of this holiday, Ray and I are sent to the French holiday camp (*colony de vacances*) with Joss, which involves being sent to France by plane with Joss, where my father meets us. Then, within a few hours, he transfers us to a train full of French children going to the holiday camp for one month. Ray and I speak no French and Joss is reluctant to look after us. We sleep in large dorms in our age and gender groups so we are all in different dorms. I worry how Ray is coping; he spends every possible minute with me. The days are a strict routine of waking at 7 a.m., making our beds, having breakfast, then visiting the horrible stinky "hole in the ground" toilets, activities until lunchtime, a two-hour siesta after lunch, which is achingly boring as we have to lie silently on our beds, activities until dinner, free time after dinner, then, finally, bed.

'Ray is the youngest child there and, one day, someone has an attack of diarrhoea all over the toilet floor. The director insists that the culprit owns up and keeps us all in after siesta. He decides it must have been Ray and Joss is sent to speak to him and me, but he insists it wasn't him. Joss tries to persuade him to admit it as she seems acutely embarrassed that he is supposedly responsible for keeping everybody in their beds. I insist that it wasn't him and that we mustn't capitulate. It feels like she is furious with me for the rest of the holiday because she hardly speaks to me.

'We return to Summerhill for the autumn term of our second year (we have spent about two weeks with our mother in the last five or so months). My mother, because she now lives locally, begins to visit us almost weekly. This isn't always a good thing because she comes into my dorm and lies on my bed, because her back aches, and "entertains" my friends. On one visit, she brings a tape recorder and says to me in front of my friends: "I've got something for you to listen to." We are all intrigued and ask her to press play.

'Intense humiliation then follows because it is me singing (in our old house I had used to pretend I was a singer and record my self). I shout at her to turn it off, but she laughs and holds it high in the air so I can't get at it. I scream louder for her to turn it off, but she continues holding the machine high above her head, so I lunge at her and manage to push her over (she falls on to a bed). I then run out of the room and hide crying in the back of her car. She finally finds me (ages later) and says: "Don't be silly. It was only a bit of fun" and then leaves, even though I plead with her to take me with her. My friends tell me I was horrible to my mother and won't speak to me for a while.'

I was red with anger while asking desperately: 'Why would she do that to me?'

'It's difficult for you to realise that your mother had little understanding for your feelings?'

'Maybe she hated me.' I aggressively asserted.

'Well, it's complicated and probably has more to do with how she felt towards her younger sister than you. The most important thing for you to know is that your mother was not able to fulfil your needs as a child because of her problems, causing you considerable pain. You were not a difficult child.' Those last few words filled me with a deep sadness that enveloped the room. I retreated to staring at my picture then abruptly resumed my narrative in a monotonous tone.

'The Christmas holidays come and we are in a couple of rented rooms in a woman's house. The rooms are very dark and scary and the woman horrible. My sister sits in the dark living room, looking hopeless and sad, smoking endless cigarettes. My mother did try to do Christmas "as usual" with stockings, which my brother and I opened very noisily at about 3 a.m. My mother has a huge row with the woman the next day and we are thrown out. Joss goes to a friend's and we (Ray, Mother and I) spent New Year in a hotel. We also end up at the Samaritans. We're in a dingy room and my mother is sobbing. I have my arm around Ray. I look towards my mother, my eyes filling with tears. She sees me and gasps: "Oh don't be upset" and turns back to the woman, sobbing.

'It is now a relief to get back to the familiarity of Summerhill and I develop a passion again for playing Mummies and Daddies, which I play constantly, but sometimes there are few willing participants. There seem to be hours at a time when no adults are around, though Ena (the headmaster's wife) sometimes comes around looking for us and has chats with us. I like her a lot, although she threatens to put me over her knee when she finds me smoking.

'Ena cannot stand my mother. I can tell because if Ena speaks to my mum her face becomes hard and angry. I think it is because Ena often finds me waiting at the gates because my mum has said she would visit but is so often very late. She is not contrite; just a casual, "Oh, you know how it is" as an excuse.

'The Easter holidays have arrived and my mother has managed to find a flat at the top of a nine-floor block of flats with no lift. However, she can't have us with her as she is working and asks Ena to keep us at school over the Easter holidays. According to my mother, Ena is incredibly rude to her and has no understanding of her situation. My mother does her usual strategy and advertises for someone to look after us in their home. Luckily a kind couple with an only son about my age (nine years old) who run a farm answer the ad so we (me and my brother, as Joss stayed with some friends) spend that three-week holiday on a farm. I like the "farmer man" but the "farmer woman" doesn't like me much because I don't like being in the kitchen with her but want to be in the fields with my brother and the boy, where they get to ride on the tractor. I plead and plead to be let out to the fields but am told angrily that "girls' work is in the house". The kitchen is dark, quiet and slow and I have to be the cook's help. I am furious that Ray is having a good time without me.

'During this time my mother has to take me to the dentist as my teeth are rotting. I have a few teeth out and remember trying to run away but being grabbed and held down by the nurse and dentist while they forced the rubber mask, smelling rubbery and awful, over my nose and mouth. I awake with blood pouring out of my mouth and my jaw throbbing like hell. I am lying in the back of my mother's car and she is taking me back to the farm. I cry hysterically and beg her not to take me back. She reluctantly takes me back to her flat for one night. I'm then back at the farm and the pain at night is very uncomfortable and I dribble blood all over the pillow, which frightens me.

'The farm then becomes an exciting place as calving begins. I love the "baby cows" and spend all my free time sneaking into the barn to stroke them and let them suck at my hand but what I don't understand is that they are waiting to be taken to be sold and have been separated from their mothers. One day, I am allowed to go and fetch the cows with the kind farmer man but I can't understand why one particular cow is at the front of the herd, practically running back to the farm, mooing loudly. The farmer man explains that she can hear her baby in the barn and wants to be reunited with her. Then the calf is put in the back of the lorry, her mother mooing frantically in the distance: I turn to farmer man asking: "Why can't you let the baby cow stay with its mother?" as I stifle a sob.

'The kind farmer man looks directly at me, with watery eyes, and replies: "That's just the way it is."'

'He was a lovely kind man to me and I have never forgotten his gentle eyes,' I murmured softly.

After a calm silence, Vida reflected: 'You had an adult who understood you.'

'Yes, but I was only with him for the Easter holidays.' My hopeless deadness enfolded me and my thoughts returned to the next summer holidays.

'We spend a couple of weeks in the flat with my mother, then are going to another *colony de vacances* but just Ray and me, not with Joss. Our time in the flat is even more boring than Summerhill, as Mum is at work and we are left in the flat all day. Ray often goes to the amusement arcades but I don't as I find all the noise and flashing lights horrible. I do sometimes go down to the beach but it's very crowded and I'm very aware that I'm the only child alone. It actually comes as a relief to be sent away to France. My father picks us up from the flat to drive us to Paris and on the way we stop at his elder son's house. Jacques is about fifteen years older than Ray and me and has a wife. We arrive in the evening and I feel Jacques looking at me with intense anger and dislike (not knowing why) and it makes me feel horrible. My father doesn't notice and acts as if everything is fine but I know different.

'It is a relief to leave early the next morning and we arrive at the colony two days later. It is very restrictive compared to Summerhill and we still can't really understand what people are saying and rely on some of the adults being able to speak a little English. When we go swimming to the sea, the "monitors" (our carers) put a rectangle of floats in the sea and we can only swim in that area, which is small and very crowded with children. I feel like I'm imprisoned and am always sneaking under the floats just to feel free. They begin to realise that I will keep doing it and threaten not to let me swim at all. Ray has very long hair, which is considered very unusual in France and one day I sit down to dinner and someone shouts: "Look at the girl" and there stands my brother on a chair looking as if he's about to sob, with his hair in bunches, holding a monitor's hand. I rush towards them, grab my brother's hand and run to the bedrooms. The director comes to find us and apologises, saying: "It was just a bit of fun."

'Shortly after this, we start to have problems with food. Ray and I are quite adamant that we won't eat horsemeat and the director decides that we must eat it and tries to insist that we eat it. During one meal, we continue to refuse the meat and, at the end of the meal, he marches us to his office with the plates of meat and says: "You will sit there until you eat it."

'We sit quietly in front of our food, not touching it. Finally, he gets really angry and gets the fork and presses it to my mouth but I close it very tightly. The director then throws the fork down and runs out of the room. Ray mumbles: "Oh let's just eat it." I refuse and a few minutes later another member of staff comes in and takes us back to our evening activities and food is never mentioned again.

'Then a bug starts to make most of us ill and the nurse decides everybody's temperature needs taking, so at siesta time we are told to remove our pants and lie down on our side and the nurse puts a thermometer up our bums. It's absolutely horrible, particularly as she only has a few thermometers in one glass full of sterilising liquid, and the disgust and humiliation I feel is very deep. The time at this camp is spent wishing for the end.

'The autumn term comes and Summerhill has become a routine that I'm used to and I've learnt to fill my time with crafts, playing and smoking. The one other delight is that my favourite woman of this year reads *The Hobbit* one evening a week to a group of us and I am transported to an underground world of strange beings and landscapes. It really scares me but I keep going to listen to more and somehow the evil monsters seem familiar.

'The Christmas holidays come and we go to the flat. Again, Ray and I are left alone a lot and fight terribly viciously, which is frightening. I try to smoke in the toilet but, as my mother doesn't smoke, she smells it and smacks me furiously. Ray and I have a particularly horrible fight so I decide that I'll run away and pack a small bag. I get about a mile away and start to feel very scared, realising I have absolutely nowhere to go, so retrace my steps back to the flat. My mother hasn't even noticed that I had left the house.

'During this holiday, a strange man comes to visit and he disappears with Mum into her bedroom while Ray and I watch TV in the living room. I feel really scared the whole time they are in the bedroom and, despite knowing about sex, don't really understand what is going on. It was also during this holiday that a woman comes from the flat below to complain about the noise (which is probably justified) and I am horrified as my mother slaps the woman across the face. The woman is speechless and leaves.'

I rested my head on my hand feeling very tired. Vida sat forward speaking quietly: 'Your time spent with your mother was very confusing and frightening.' I lifted my head to reply.

'I just can't believe everything she did to me and that she still maintained that she loved me.' I returned heavily to my story.

'We're back at Summerhill and Mum visits much less often. During this term, I have a very clear memory of seeing *Top of the Pops* on the TV for the first time. Marc Bolan is singing and I'm mesmerised by the man and the music. We sometimes put music on in the hall, usually the Beatles, and all dance. I am entranced by dancing, and one day a sixth form girl (who frightens me) asks me: "Where did you learn to dance like that? You're really good." It's not often I hear someone saying that I'm good at something and the feeling of being noticed stays with me.

'The summer term comes and we spend time in the open-air pool whenever possible which is open nearly every day so we just swim and swim and, being at a "free" school we swim naked! Swimming naked is such a glorious feeling for me, something about the water gliding gently uninterrupted across every bit of my skin. My mother and Joss visit us for one day and take us out for a picnic in a rowing boat but, as we attempt to stop by the side, to have our picnic on the river bank, I lose my footing getting out of the boat and fall in the river. My mother and Joss think this is hilarious and continue to laugh at me, without helping me, as I struggle to get out of the water. I am very upset and run away and lie in the grass crying. They don't follow me and after a long while I return and they don't ask me anything about why I ran away (there is also no food left for me).

'The summer holidays arrive. My father has arranged for my mother, sister, brother and me to go to a Club Med for a month. I am pleased that we're not going to a *colony de vacances* but, after we have arrived, Mum expects Ray and me to go to the "Kid's Club" and is surprised when we refuse. It doesn't seem to enter her mind that we've just come from Summerhill and have not spent any time with her or Joss. We don't see Joss for the whole time, as she is quite happy to become a twenty-four-hour member of the Club Med Teen Club.

'The sea is fantastic and I enjoy playing around with Ray, as we don't make friends easily. We also play a lot of ping pong but the tension builds between Mother, Ray and me and we have vicious fights. Mum would often refer to the fact that, at the end of the holiday, she had just finished packing the suitcase when I, in a rage, emptied the contents all over the floor.

'We return to Summerhill for the autumn term and a new dorm. In the new dorm we each have a shelf allocated to us and one girl has a shelf full of model horses. Towards the end of the term one of the horses goes missing, which causes a huge drama.

A girl accuses me of stealing it (I haven't) and manages to convince all the other girls in our dorm that I have stolen it and Kathy decides that they should send me to Coventry until I give it back. It's my first experience of being ignored by so many people and it's very scary and if I had the horse I'd certainly give it back but I don't and it doesn't matter what I say because nobody will believe me.

'Their determination to not speak to me goes on until the end of term so I am very relieved to go to the flat for the Christmas holidays and towards the end of this holiday I have a hysterical outburst in front of my mother telling her that I won't go back to Summerhill. She does ask me why but I can't tell her because I think she'll tell me I'm being ridiculous. My mother despairs of what to do with me and phones the headmaster at Joss's boarding school and pleads with him to take me. He agrees, so I go to Summerhill to collect my things and leave with great relief, and am put on the train with Joss to Menton School.'

I sat breathlessly looking at Vida, directly into her beautiful brown eyes. Vida readjusted her body while beginning to speak: 'You were now having to deal with yet another change to your school and carers. You had so many different carers in your early childhood that it might have been better for you if you'd been adopted.' I was lost for words and left the session feeling dizzy and confused.

My routine with Simon and the children marched on relentlessly; evenings filled with children playing, homework, cooking meals and bedtime stories. Since being in therapy, Simon and I had generally become better parents through having loads of discussions about our own childhoods and what we want for our children, though it would often feel like taking one step forward and two back because we'd have yet another terrible argument, usually about how Simon was too harsh with our children or when I was not firm enough in sticking to saying 'no'. Gradually, these episodes were becoming less frequent, but I longed for them to stop.

It didn't help that Simon had been in the house for nearly three and a half years before finally being offered a job in his old department. In a later session, I began telling Vida my good news: 'Simon has been offered a job but I can't believe it; he's not yet accepted it.'

Vida smiled so broadly her whole face was radiant. 'That's such good news, what is the job and why has he not accepted it?'

I aggressively crossed my legs and folded my arms. 'It's not what he wanted and, he's right; it is only an eighteen month contract and the pay is awful but I don't see what choice he's got. After all it's better than the dole and it might lead on to something. I just feel exasperated at his hesitation and I'm scared the job offer will be withdrawn.'

'It sounds to me like you are right and he should take the job,' Vida said, leaning forward reassuringly. I shifted awkwardly in my chair.

'Well, I'll just have to hope he makes the right decision because there's nothing else I can say to him.'

'You have waited a long time for him to get some stable work', Vida reflected back to me the obvious. I was pushed into my ocean of staring, making me float off out of my surroundings into an endless fluffy cloud of nothing. When I became aware of my thoughts again, I was arriving at my new boarding school.

'Menton School is an old mansion house made of beautiful, creamy, rusty, orange-coloured sandstone, such a contrast to Summerhill, which was a large squarish building in dull red brick. The entrance to Menton is one mile from the house and, as you drive up the mature tree-lined road, it gradually comes into view and is stunning set against a lush landscape of trees, clipped lawns and flowering borders. The front of the house has a huge porch with four sandstone pillars supporting a terrace from the first floor and leads to a majestic wooden door with a large brass door-knocker.

'The house is beautifully balanced, with three floors of rooms looking out from five windows overlooking the sports field, and the stunning countryside beyond, of tended fields of crops and farm animals. I am entranced by this house; it is like how I imagine the house of a prince would be. I just love the space and elegance and it makes me feel like a princess just being there. The back of the house has the old stable blocks, which have been converted to classrooms, the rest of the boys' wing, more staff rooms and toilets and washrooms. At the left side of the house are tended gardens and lawns, tennis courts and an outdoor swimming pool. Behind the old stables and garden buildings are two winding paths that lead to a huge magical wood of mature oak and other deciduous trees.

'My first memory is of standing alone on the landing next to my dorm, feeling all panicky with a tummy ache and a queasy feeling. In the first days, Joss takes me aside and explains to me that I now have to refer to Dad as "Uncle", because the French teacher knows him and Dad doesn't want any of his work colleagues or friends knowing about his illegitimate family. I find this quite hard and often make mistakes but eventually I even write letters to "Uncle Louis" and he doesn't ever protest.

'My dorm is on the first floor and has about twelve girls aged about twelve and one sixth former. We have bunk beds and I have a top bunk. The bathroom is adjacent, with one bath and one toilet. I particularly hate queuing for the toilet in the mornings and the fact that the toilet has a flimsy partition means that everyone knows exactly what is happening. I find this acutely embarrassing so I try to sneak back upstairs after breakfast to have some quiet time alone (we aren't allowed in our dorms after breakfast and all day). In the evenings, trying to get a bath is difficult and girls often end up two or three to the bath (I also find this embarrassing).

'Bullying is common. One night (at my suggestion) we decide to fill an unpopular girl's pillow case with grass and thistles and after she gets into bed and puts her head down she holds her tears back and quietly removes the pillow. I feel so awful I decide then never to have anything to do with group bullying again.

'I don't like much of the food, particularly Sunday breakfast, which is disgusting, with fried eggs floating in horrible smelling oil. I often feel hungry, particularly in the evenings because we have our tea at 5 p.m. then no food is provided until breakfast; food is a big issue for all of us. However, some staff members regularly have us into their rooms, in the evenings and at weekends, for a hot drink and biscuits.

'I don't make new friends easily and during the first weeks I spend all my spare time with Joss and her friends. She is part of a group of about four boys and two girls and the teenage boys give me shoulder and piggy back rides and generally play rough and tumble games with me. I can't figure out why Joss allows me to 'tag along' with her and her friends; it confuses me because it feels like an act of kindness yet that isn't her usual behaviour. Joss can also be very strange at times, filling me with feelings of confusion and hurt. Mum phones us on the pupil payphone and one time Joss says: "Get out. I want to talk to Mum" and pushes me out of the booth. As she comes out, I ask what it was about, to which she replies in a triumphant sarcastic tone: "It's none of your business." The pleasure she takes in excluding me is obvious in her smiling swaggering walk and reminds me of this aspect of our relationship that I hate.

'A particular joy for me is being back in the classroom until it dawns on me how much I don't know; my writing and spelling are still that of a seven year old and maths causes me so much frustration I sometimes cry. I try so hard, at first, to concentrate and work, but in the end I can't deal with the huge gaps in my knowledge and understanding, so I begin to mess around in class and play truant. I do try to improve my handwriting by endlessly copying neat writing. A letter written by me to my father at this time talks proudly of how my handwriting now "looks like Joss's". I also try to learn the times tables but again I only have some success and can't sustain the concentration needed. I do enjoy cookery, sewing, pottery, woodwork, history (the teacher is a very kind woman) and French, so I only tend to play truant from English, sciences, geography and maths.

'During this term I have my first taste of cider and being drunk and I love it. Each weekend becomes a quest to find the money to buy some booze (cider and barley wine being the favourites) and then to get an older person to buy the booze and fags for us from the village. I always try to get to the point of not caring about anything because, if I don't drink enough, I start to sob, not really knowing about what, and I am often violently sick. I have visible black holes in my canine teeth and I have to visit the dentist for fillings in the back teeth, which I dread. Luckily, the holes in my canines were in my first teeth (I was late in losing my first teeth) and, while smoking a cigarette with Gabby and Mary, I bite hard on the tip of the fag and one of my black teeth comes out, stuck to the fag end. This looks very odd and makes us laugh for ages. I am very proud of my new gap and very relieved to see the ugly tooth gone and am persuaded by the biology teacher to put it under my pillow for the tooth fairy. Although I think it is silly, I decide to play along, as the teacher is usually kind. To my delight, and great surprise, I awake the next morning to find that the tooth fairy has visited and has not only left some money but a whole mixed bag of bracelets, money, fruit and sweets.'

Vida seemed tired as she looked at me but she still managed to give me some of her thoughts. 'It sounds like your new school was able to give you more than Summerhill despite your difficulties in making friends.' I tried to sound enthusiastic.

'Yes, I think my education did, despite the problems, begin again after the long three years at Summerhill, which gave me a sense of purpose rather than the total sense of the futility of my existence that I often had felt at Summerhill. It's incredible how the kindness of a few can rekindle hope for better things and obliterate other people's nastiness. I can feel now how the 'tooth fairy' built on the kindness of other adults I had met, through foster care and at Summerhill, and strengthened my faith that there were kind people in the world who would think of me.'

Another session was over, and I felt unsure of whether Vida was becoming bored of my ramblings. The week passed, as usual, and I was back in my chair, Vida smiling at me, asking: 'How are you?'

This question made me feel awkward and my usual reply was 'crap', 'shit' or 'fucked', though recently I had managed to elaborate by saying: 'I feel depressed and tired.' After a small pause, I re-launched my boarding school narrative.

'The spring school holidays come and are initially great because Mum has moved back to our old house; it is so wonderful to be back in the house I feel is my home but it is also disappointing because it isn't the same. The house and garden have been rubbished by the people who had rented it and we have lost all our friends. I am very happy to return to Menton for the summer term; I really enjoy the beautiful grounds and woods and, on hot sunny days, the outdoor pool.

'Eventually I do make a close friendship with two girls, Gabby and Mary, from the form above. I find out later that Gabby's sister has been badly bullied by Joss and that she has deliberately enticed me away from my sister in order "to get her back". She is very moody and bossy and gets me to run errands for her. I am quite frightened of her and want to make sure she doesn't get cross with me so "happily" do what she wants me to do. We get drunk together (me having paid for the booze because I can write to my parents and get them to send me the odd fiver) and smoke together. We occasionally have fun together trying to play tennis or walking into the village, which we are allowed to do at the weekends. I love walking down the tree-lined drive in the warm summer sun, dawdling along, chatting and laughing with Gabby and Mary, but it is a drag when we get to the road as it is another mile to walk. It is around this time I get my own gerbil, which lives in "Pets' Corner", and I visit her daily to hold her and feed her and I am amazed because she seems to recognise me.'

I looked up to see Vida's eyes almost closed so I immediately asked: 'Am I boring you?'

Her body jerked up, her eyes widened, and she said in an angry tone: 'No. Why do you think you're boring?'

I was stunned into a silence because I wasn't used to hearing her speak to me like that. We sat in an uncomfortable silence and to avoid it lasting any longer I rushed on.

'The summer holidays are spent at another *colony de vacances* (even though I have told my parents I hate them). My father takes us out in Paris before our journeys south or back to England and this time he brings Fabienne (a French woman friend of his who he occasionally brought with him) and she is heavily pregnant. On the way home, Joss says to us (Ray and me) in an intense and angry voice: "Don't you dare tell Mum." I am confused and we don't talk about it further. We return home and I can hardly speak to my mother so, a few days after being with her, I carefully say to her: "Promise you won't tell who told you", to which she replies casually that she won't. I then say, heart thumping, with a shaky voice: "Dad was with a lady who's going to have a baby."

'My mother turns violently towards me and grabs my hand roughly and screams: "Are you sure?" I nod my head slowly but she says again: "You promise me you are sure?"

'I shout: "Yes, yes", nearly bursting into tears.

'At this point my mother collapses on to the floor shaking her head, then turns to me with a fixed expression of fury, and asks me: "Exactly how and where have you met this woman?" I tell her that I first met her at Summerhill and how sometimes we had seen her in France.'

I looked towards Vida, whose eyes were now wide open, and with a shaky voice, told her: 'By the end of my description, my mother looked white and inanimate and I now wonder if she had still been hoping that my father would marry her. How could my father have had a baby with another woman when we needed him so much? Had I been still hoping that he would leave his wife and marry my mum and look after us?' I immediately turned towards my picture and sank into staring at a faraway place. Vida cleared her throat, shifted around in her chair noisily and began to speak.

'You were about to have a new half-sister or brother to another woman and your father thought it OK for him to not tell you, or your sister and brother, himself. Even worse was his allowing you, your sister and brother to carry this burden without your mother knowing.'

'How could he tell us that he loved us? I hate him for what he did to all of us and, if he were alive, I'd murder him.'

Vida breathed slowly, while in a soothing tone, she told me: 'You are feeling enraged by your father's persistent lack of care for you and your sister, brother and mother.' I suddenly remembered a time with my father when I was in my early twenties.

'When I am in my early twenties I spend a couple of days in Paris with my father. After taking me to the Palace of Versailles, we go for lunch in a lovely buzzing café. During the lunch, he turns to me and says in a fast, casual manner: "I'm sorry about your childhood but there's nothing I can do now as it's too late." As he says the words "too late", he slapped his hands on his knees, which I think means: "Thank goodness I've got that out of the way, now we can forget it and move on".'

I turned quickly towards Vida, words tumbling forcefully from my mouth. 'I, as usual, said nothing and now I wish I had slapped him in his face and said: "Is that all I'm worth: a flippant apology for my whole childhood, you arrogant bastard?" and then I should have walked away from him.' I sat in my chair, shaking with pent-up rage and Vida gently spoke to me.

'Yes, your father's apology was very hurtful towards you because, by not having an open discussion with you and offering some actions to try to make amends, he belittled the pain he had caused you by his neglectful parenting.'

I left the session feeling a hatred for my father that was all-consuming and I had images in my head of me stabbing myself over and over in my chest and stomach, blood gushing from my injured body. The pain of his disregard for me was unbearable. The sight of my children brought me back; the love I feel for them prevented me from becoming completely self-destructive.

Chapter 7

Simon did take the job, which was such a relief. At last he was out of the house in the week and we had slightly more money, though he continued to look for other jobs so I wasn't released from the unsettling thoughts of possible house and school changes. I had managed to make friends with a couple of women (mothers of my children's friends) and we had begun to meet at each other's houses for dinner parties (with husbands) and, although I found them very difficult (making conversation was not easy, I would either be completely tongue-tied or gush about some heavy, controversial political issue), I was beginning to feel that I was achieving my aim of a 'normal' life. This was helped by me nearing the end of my counselling diploma, which I thought would lead to a long-term settled career, and my children were doing much better at school and had nice friends. I was back in Vida's comforting presence and had still not finished telling her about my time at Menton.

'I return to school for the autumn term alone because Joss has left the school to go to a day school for her sixth form. I am in a new dorm with a bed that is not a bunk, which gives me a great sense of freedom because in my own bed I can move around as much as I want and not be woken by the bed shaking from someone else's movements. There are three new girls in our dorm and I particularly like Lilly (though I'm not really aware of it). She's from London, has fabulous Mary Quant clothes and she is very pretty with high cheekbones, marble-smooth skin, a small, beautifully shaped mouth, warm, gentle, brown eyes and black, tightly curled hair. She also has a woman's body, with very large, wonderfully shaped breasts held on her slim delicate frame. I have never met anyone like her before and I am amazed that she seems happy to talk to me and even lend me her clothes; she has a beautiful swishy long white cotton skirt with tiny purple flowers on that I borrow (as much as I can). Gabby and Mary are still the girls who I hang out with most of the time (because I don't know how to get away from them) though I would have liked to spend more time with Lilly.

'I then get a taste of Gabby's nastiness when she decides that I have been talking about her behind her back (twisting what I had said) and sends me to Coventry. She seems to have the power to get all the girls in my form and her form not to speak to me and suddenly my world is filled with confusion and terrible hurt. I can't believe this is happening to me again and phone my mum in tears. She phones the headmaster but he seems to do nothing other than have a talk with me and tell me to keep my chin up and that it will soon blow over. It seems to go on for days and, at times, is very frightening. I am in my dorm sitting on my bed and they all crowd around me, with Gabby at the front, telling me that I should "admit what I said". I react by staring fixedly at a mark on the wall, making my body completely dead and floppy, and I float away until they are very distant from me, to the extent that I seem not to hear them any more. They go on and on and start to bash a stick close to me on my bed but still I remain fixed in the same position. Eventually, Gabby turns and leaves and everybody follows. I then lie down in my bed with the covers over my head and go to sleep. After about ten days, I bump into Gabby and I take the opportunity to apologise for "upsetting her", though I hadn't meant to. She accepts and suddenly everyone is speaking to me again.'

I looked towards Vida with desolation. 'I couldn't believe that this was happening to me again. My happiness was now gone. I was guarded and frightened of being ostracised, particularly as it seemed to happen so easily and I didn't really understand how it had happened. Why was life so shit to me?' I left no time for Vida's response.

'After this time, I know that I hate Gabby and try to spend less time with her but she always seems to seek me out. I get very frustrated and decide that I hate the school and that I'll run away back to my home. I tell a couple of girls from my dorm and surprisingly Katie, who I don't really get on with, insists on coming with me. We leave after breakfast and walk the back way to the village (so as not to be seen) and, about halfway there, Katie stops and tries to persuade me to go back but I am absolutely determined to go home so we carry on to the village where I get money out of my post office account to pay for the bus. I actually quite enjoy the walk with Katie and feel quite strange (I think now it was about feeling cared for in a way that was unusual for me and perhaps Katie was much more mature than me and was genuinely trying to make some sort of amends for being part of the group sending me to Coventry).

'We have to take two buses, with an hour to wait at a large bus station for our connection. When we get there, we don't have any money to go to the café and we haven't eaten for a few hours so we just hang around outside, looking longingly at what people are eating. As we are staring through the window, a man comes and asks us if we are hungry and offers to buy us a meal. Katie holds back but I, naively, rush towards him nodding. We enter the café and have egg and chips with the man asking us what we are doing alone. He then offers to drive us to my house, at which point we get quite scared and both Katie and I refuse. We run out of the café and decide it would be safest to go into the phone box and phone my mum.

'I get through to her and tell her what has happened and she tells me that she will pick me up from the bus when we arrive and not to be silly and tell stories about things when I mention the man. The man seems to hang around for ages looking at us but we just stay in the phone box, pretending to talk to someone until he went.

'We both get on the bus, very relieved and my mum is there when we arrive. I don't have any conversation with my mother and, half an hour after we arrive at my house, my father turns up to drive us back to school (not asking why I had tried to come home). This event does seem to restore my trust in my friends from my form and I quickly settle back into school and spend less and less time with Gabby and more time with the two other new girls, Chloe and Cathy. I would prefer to spend more time with Lilly but she has a boyfriend and spends most of her time with him even though he can be a real nasty bastard to her by humiliating her in front of us; I can't understand why she still goes out with him.

'Chloe and Cathy are both quiet and shy girls and I don't have a strong affinity with either of them but we have no one else and they, for some reason that I don't understand, seem to really like me, particularly Cathy. The three of us often sneak down to the cellar (the sixth form common room) and make coffee and they often listen to music that I find really exciting but sometimes the music touches a deep longing in me that makes me feel like dying. We also spend a lot of time hanging out after meals at the pond in the woods with all the smokers, who are from all the different age groups. I have a comforting routine at last! The Christmas holidays come and I become agitated and panicky again and this time is worse because my mother has moved to a house in a tree-less road. This small house is in a grim and run-down area of town in a brick terrace with no front garden and a tiny back garden.'

My eyes reached out towards Vida. 'The house was in chaos and Ray and I shared a bedroom with bunk beds (I was twelve years old). We didn't know anybody and my mother spent her days in bed with her bad back. It was an endless time of boredom; no outings, no visitors, just TV and fights with Ray. How could my mother ignore us like this?' Vida shifted in her chair, with deliberate movements.

'You often felt you were a burden on your mother?' I stared at the bright green leaves on the shaking branch of my tree. It occasionally knocked against the window and my thoughts then returned to the summer holidays.

'The summer holidays are looming and my mother casually tells me that there will be no one to look after Zircon, a pet rabbit of mine that I love. I don't protest as I know it will be useless and start to ask around if anybody would have him because I decide it is best to find him a home where he will be looked after properly. I am getting desperate because no one is interested but then Lilly offers and I am so pleased because I know she is kind.

'The summer holidays come and Ray and I are going on another *colony de vacances* and we have to stay in London one night on the way and Lilly agrees to let us stay at her house. We arrive at her house at midday and it is amazing; a huge terraced building in the centre of London. The living room has a lovely polished wood floor, covered with gorgeous patterned rugs. It has very high ceilings and the walls are covered with abstract and still life paintings and the room is furnished with an assortment of interestingly covered and cushioned armchairs and sofas. Lilly's mother is also very beautiful and speaks with a soft gentle voice and she cooks the most fantastic meal that evening. I have never tasted a food like it. She makes some sort of meat in a creamy sauce, and I just keep asking for more and she does get irritated but I still wish so much that she was my mum. In the evening, a crowd of Lilly's mum's friends come and they share their grass with us. I feel so warm and so special to be included (Lilly's parents are divorced so I don't get to meet her dad). I also get to see Zircon and feel so happy that he is with them and I don't miss him (maybe I feel a bit of me was with Lilly and her family).'

I spoke with a great longing: 'I wished so much that I had a mum like Lilly's and a house like theirs, so interesting and warm.' Vida sat silently looking gently into my eyes. I began to feel uncomfortable and continued.

'On the way to the holiday camp, we meet my father's new baby, Cecile. I love babies and can't help loving her. She is six months old when I meet her and very cuddly and smiley and I just adore being with her. Fabienne is a very caring mother and she is also very kind to Ray and I, seeming to be genuinely interested in us; she gives us much more attention than we are used to getting from either of our parents.'

'I had met another woman who I longed to be my mother', I wistfully told Vida.

'You were beginning to understand how much your mother and father neglected you', Vida's voice quietly insisted. I returned to Menton.

'Ray is now at Menton. I am expected to look after him, which is OK up to a point but, as my mother has asked me to stop using the laundry service (it was too expensive), it means that each weekend I spend a lot of time in the washroom, washing Ray's and my clothes. Ray is having problems making friends and I am sure it doesn't help that he can hardly write because he's had virtually no formal education yet he is eleven years old. I manage to write to Mum, asking her to get some extra tutoring for Ray (which she does) so he starts to get some help but he still doesn't make friends easily and gets into fights. A particular fight becomes very vicious. I manage to split them up, and Ray runs off into the woods. I run after him and find him lying crying on the ground so I sit next to him and he puts his head in my lap and sobs for a long time. I am nearly crying with him but hold back because I feel I have to be strong for him and sit silently with him until he falls quiet in my arms.'

Tears were threatening to flow. I swallowed. 'I felt so desperate for us and I just cannot understand how my parents allowed our education to be so awful. After all, my father was now a senior lecturer at an English university, taught at the Sorbonne in Paris and had written several academic books and, although my mother couldn't hold down a job because of her back problems, she was educated to degree level. How could they have done that to my brother? He's never regained his education (he left school with no exams and took an apprenticeship).' We sat together in a sad silence and I returned to my history.

'This year, my father begins to visit us regularly and I look forward to his Saturday or Sunday visit because he takes us out to a café, where we can order what we like, and then he takes us to the local supermarket to stock up on goodies to take back to school and, although we aren't supposed to have food in our dorms, we all hide it in our lockers. I love cream cheese on crackers and buy loads to share it with my friends in the evenings after lights-out. He also gives us money so I often have cash to buy fags and booze. My mother occasionally visits but my strongest memory is waiting and waiting at the end of the drive because, as usual, she is much later than she has said.

'The summer term is great because, during the last few weeks, we are allowed to camp on the front garden and Lilly agrees to share a tent with me; I'm so thrilled. The first few nights are great and we talk together before we drop off to sleep but then she starts to leave to be with her boyfriend so I'm left for most of the night on my own. One night, I have a terrifying nightmare involving an old man chasing me, wanting to really hurt me. I awake at the point of him nearly catching me and, knowing that I'll never escape him, I am drenched in sweat and shaking with absolute terror. I am convinced that he is somewhere outside the tent so I quickly open the tent and run like mad back to the house and the comforting presence of my sleeping dorm-mates. I don't camp out after this and never talk about my dream.

'My father visits us for the last time that term and casually asks me if I'd like to go to school in France next year. It's the first I've heard about leaving Menton, but I respond without thinking, "yes". The decision is taken for the next school year; Ray is to go to a day school and live with my mother and I am to go to live in France with my father's third family (Fabienne and Cecile), though my father only spends weekends with them because he remains married to his wife.'

I gazed silently at my favourite picture and Vida's gentle tones broke through my oasis of floaty nothingness. 'You were being moved to yet another school, home and carers, which must have been very difficult for you to cope with.' Another session ended and I felt numb with exhaustion but somehow managed to drive home. My head spun, trying to keep track of my childhood life, yet I was driven to try to get it into some sort of order and spent my next sessions telling Vida about my year spent living in Paris when I was thirteen and a half years old.

'I arrive in Paris with my father. It has taken a whole day to get here as we've come by car and ferry. His wife and Celine (his third legitimate child and my older half-sister) travel with us because my father is on sabbatical for the next two terms and they are going to live in their Paris home. I know that Celine is my half-sister but, as she does not, I am introduced to her as a daughter of one of my father's colleagues. Apparently my father's wife, Celine's mother, has forbidden Louis (I never refer to him as "Dad" anymore) to tell Celine until she is old enough to take it (she is now nearly sixteen years old)! The journey is very tense because I can never bear deception and I have to be quite reserved with "Uncle Louis" so as not to seem "too familiar"! Celine does question me on how I knew him, to which I respond: "He's my Uncle."

'She looks startled and says: "But that's impossible because he's an only child" so I mumbled something about him being such close friends with my dad that he was like an uncle.'

I was laughing as I told Vida: 'It was completely ridiculous but she didn't question me further.' Vida did not return my mirth and had her most serious face while sharing her thoughts with me.

'Yes, it was ridiculous and also completely insensitive to your feelings; your father seemed to have little capacity to see what he did to those he claimed to love.' My smile dropped from my face and I suddenly saw myself through Vida's eyes. I couldn't tolerate the pain of my father's blindness to me and rejoined my stay in Paris.

'We finally enter Paris and, after dropping off Celine and her mother at their flat, we drive to Fabienne's. Her flat is on the second floor of a new curved building, not far from the centre of the city. It is very small with only two bedrooms, one living room with a balcony, a tiny kitchen and an even smaller bathroom and toilet. Fabienne's elderly father lives with her and has one of the bedrooms. Fabienne, Cecile and my father have the second bedroom, and I am to sleep in the living room on the sofa that converts into a bed. My clothes are to be kept in a small wardrobe in Fabienne's bedroom; this is the only space for my possessions because the living room has no space for anything else.

'This is to be my new home for the next nine months (I do go back to England in the holidays) and I feel very claustrophobic in the first days but I love playing with Cecile who is now a charming friendly eighteen-month-old who enjoys all the attention I give her. My first day at the lycee is about ten days after my arrival and my father takes me along, introduces me to a teacher and leaves. I still am not fluent in French so struggle in the first few weeks to communicate but most of the children in my year are very interested in me and look after me well. I can hardly recall not being able to communicate with people and within a few weeks I must become quite fluent. Fabienne and her father (Charles) can only speak a few English words, which means that I am completely immersed in the language.

'My father spends the week living with Fabienne and goes to his wife and Celine at the weekends, leaving me with Fabienne, Cecile and Charles. Charles is quite funny and teaches me magic card tricks and takes me with him to his café. Charles is also a wonderful cook, particularly of soups and makes them regularly. I have lots of bowls of his warming soup. Fabienne often does the evening meals, which are simple but so much better than I've had previously. She usually cooks some meat with salad or pasta and I begin to enjoy food in a way that I haven't often experienced. I also love the *boulangeries* and *patisseries* and stop after school each day and usually buy a *chausson au pomme* (flaky pastry with apple puree in the middle) and get some *croissants au buerre* for breakfast the next day. Fabienne also decides that my clothes are dreadful (my mother has long since stopped taking me to buy clothes and I have shopped for myself in the last couple of years) and takes me shopping to buy me a fantastic assortment of trousers (I never wear skirts), shirts, jumpers and a lovely new coat. She also takes me to a jewellery shop and asks me to choose myself a bracelet. I have never been treated with such care and am so overwhelmed I just point to the first bracelet I see, but it doesn't matter because I wear it very proudly (even though I really don't like it). She also tries to persuade me to have a new watch, as mine is an old one of my father's, but I insist that I don't need one.'

'I loved the attention she gave me and I wished she was my mother.' I quietly looked into Vida's soft, mesmerising eyes.

'She was able to see some of your needs and behaved as a caring adult towards you.' my gently spoken friend said, trying to help me face reality, yet again.

'Yes, and she taught me how to behave,' I replied enthusiastically.

'I often have a bath and forget to close the bedroom door while I am dressing (my mother embraced the sixties freedom ideology). Charles notices and Fabienne has a quiet word about me covering up and then says: *"Ton pere pense que tu va bien tot commencer tes regles"* ("your father thinks you're about to start your period"). At this I blush for ages and feel really sick that my father has been talking about me in this way. I have sort of wondered when my period might arrive but find anything to do with this aspect of life nauseating. I quickly forget about anything to do with this but do take more care in hiding my maturing body.

'I manage to find an escape through Agatha Christie murder mystery books (Fabienne has a large collection written in English) and I read book after book and in the end I can always guess who the murderer is. Eventually, I have read all of them and try to re-read them but I find it too boring. I also spend time escaping by planning how to get a smoke because I am still hooked on cigarettes and, as both Fabienne and Charles smoke, I can either nip into the toilet for a quick puff or I pretend to go to the shops and have a fag in the stairwell. It is around this time that I start to have insomnia and start to dread going to bed at night. Fabienne takes me to the doctor who prescribes a sedative, which I am very reluctant to take, and I am regularly awake for a lot of the night. I often get up in the mornings and say I am *"trop fatigue pour aller a l'ecole"* ("too tired to go to school") which Fabienne agrees to, at first, but then she insists that, unless I am ill, I should go.

'One of my problems at school is managing to understand the work. The education system in France is based on regular testing and my marks are usually very low. The teachers don't give me any leniency for the fact that I am English attending a French school for the first time and aren't aware of my previous lack of education. I start to really hate most of the lessons and dread the tests, particularly in French, where the teacher asks random questions about French grammar, which I always get wrong, as I haven't any idea what a simple verb is, let alone complicated grammatical constructions. We are also asked to learn French poems off by heart to recite to the class and I find the experience of standing up in front of the class unbearably humiliating. My school days become long stretches of time spent trying to avoid being noticed by teachers in class and longing for home time.

'During the week, my father sometimes picks me up straight from school and we go to visit his mother (my grandmother). She is quite old and frail but manages to live on her own and she doesn't know who I am, because my father introduces me as "a daughter of an English friend", which she seems to accept. It's quite weird being with my grandmother and father yet having to be a "friend's daughter" but I'm used to pretending and it doesn't stop me warming to her. I also feel sorry for her, living all alone (my grandfather died in the year I was born) and hardly seeing my father because he's usually in England.

'I also feel quite lonely because I haven't sustained the popularity that I initially had at school and spend most of my break time talking to the teachers on playground duty. At last I do get an invite to a party from a girl in my class who I dislike and, when I'm at the party, I am so shy that I can't join in the dancing and I hear the girl saying that "*l'anglaise est ennuiyeuse*" ("the English girl is boring") so back at school even fewer people talk to me.

'Fortunately, the weekends become less lonely and boring because Joss and Philippe arrive to live in Paris for a few months. I get into a routine of visiting them every weekend. It takes me about an hour and a half by metro and bus on a Saturday morning and I return to Fabienne's on a Sunday afternoon. I don't understand why they are happy to have me with them as I am only thirteen years old; it reminds me of my first weeks at Menton when Joss allowed me to hang out with her and her friends. Anyway I am very pleased to be part of their weekends, especially because they either have an exciting dinner party with friends or go out to the centre of Paris to the restaurant and cinema.

'The Christmas holidays arrive and I return to my mother's house on my own because my father, Joss and Philippe are staying in Paris. This is one of the first times I travel completely on my own on a complicated journey. I take the train from Paris to Calais, then train from Dover to London. In London I go to another station to catch my train to my mother's and I do this with a taxi. When the taxi stops to drop me off, as I go to pay, the driver says: "No, you keep it for yourself and go home."

'I protest: "No, take the money" and don't really understand what he is talking about. In the end, he takes the money but looks so sadly at me.'

'I must have looked so young and vulnerable and it makes me feel so angry and humiliated to think that my parents never saw what was obvious to a complete stranger. My mother and father didn't really see me because they were both so preoccupied with themselves; my mother with her back problems and my father with his lovers and his work. I feel that myself and Ray were some sort of irritant that they didn't know what to do with and I often wonder why my mother hadn't had the courage to have us adopted and also wonder whether our illegitimacy made us not as valuable as our legitimate siblings and parents.' I was breathless with anger and deep sadness. I left no room for Vida's thoughts.

'I arrive at the train station in my mother's town. Because she never bothers to meet me, I have yet another journey on a bus and a walk, carrying my heavy bag, down the treeless, grey street of my mother's house, then I am "home". I enter the house and no one is around because my mother is lying in bed nursing her back problems, watching TV and Ray is watching the TV in the living room (which is how he spends most of his time).
     'I return to Paris, alone, three weeks later. My father picks me up from the train station and takes me to Fabienne's and, as we open the front door, Fabienne pulls me into a big hug; I've never been hugged with such force and it overwhelms me. I am so happy to see Cecile as I have missed her joyfulness. I then find out that there has been a big change over the Christmas break; my father, in a fit of anger because he'd argued with his wife, has told Celine that she has six brothers and sisters. He has also told his mother about Cecile and takes me on her first visit to her (our) grandmother. He hasn't told my grandmother that I am also her granddaughter and I am forced to watch my grandmother trying to win over Cecile while ignoring me, "an English child of my father's colleague".'

I could not find any words and tried to get comfort from watching the gently swaying branches of my beloved tree. 'Your father's disregard for you was inexcusable', Vida said in an angry voice. I was surprised and frightened by her forcefulness and simply ran on.

'A few weekends later, instead of going to Joss's, I decide to visit my grandmother on my own and take her some flowers to plant in her outside pot that I had noticed was empty. She has cooked me her speciality potato purée which is very smooth and buttery and we laugh together as we eat. I really like being with her. I also feel very happy planting flowers for her and an exchange that is etched in my mind is when I turn towards her after we've laughed together and she says to me: "*Tu sais, tu est come moi*" ("You know, you are like me"), "*j'etais plat juste comme toi*" ("I was flat chested just like you") while she moves her arm across her chest. I don't quite understand what she's saying and am slightly embarrassed but looking back I wonder if she was trying to tell me that she saw a connection between us. As I leave, she is nearly asleep in her chair watching TV and I look back at her with tears in my eyes and remind her: "*N'oublier pas d'aroser les fleurs*" ("don't forget to water the flowers").'

I looked up towards Vida. 'I didn't ever go back to see her because I found the deception too painful and I never saw her again. However, I must have gained something from our short time together because I would often say to people proudly that I was "just like my French grandmother."'

'It sounds to me as if your grandmother knew who you were.' Vida's words brought tears to my eyes. We sat in a warm silence until it was time for Vida to look in her diary to make our next appointment. My life seemed to exist in parallel and unconnected lines; my therapy was a separate line of my life, which had its own journey, and, despite the 'interruptions' of my adult home life and holiday breaks, carried on session after session. At my next session I was still in Paris.

'My father decides it would be a very good idea to take Joss, Celine, Cecile and I out for a meal on a Saturday afternoon because of Celine's newly acquired knowledge of the existence of her half-sisters and brothers (I am very careful to emphasis the "half"). The meeting is awkward and full of long silences, punctuated by Celine saying: "This is strange." Celine pays very little attention to Cecile (in fact, she seems to deliberately be ignoring her) and spends most of her time greatly admiring my new coat (the one that Fabienne had bought for me). She later insists that my father take her to the same shop and buy her one and I am cross because I don't like the idea of her wearing the same coat as me (I soon stop wearing mine and she has hers for years). My father doesn't suggest another meeting between the four of us and I go back to my routine of visiting Joss at the weekends.

'Things are going better for me at school because I have made friends with a girl I really like called Sylvie. She hasn't many friends (although I wasn't aware at the time, I wonder if it was because she was half Tunisian). She is very pretty and invites me to her small flat after school where we talk, eat and play games together. We are often alone because her mother works and is divorced from her father. Some weekends, instead of going to Joss's, I now spend with Sylvie, going to the cinema and having dinner with her and her mother. We really enjoy being with each other and are often in fits of giggles together and school isn't lonely any more because we spend all our break times together and sometimes go back to her flat for lunch, though we nearly fall out because I did something very strange in front of her mother.

'Sylvie and I had been to the cinema together and her mother was asking about the film and then said: "*Est-ce qu'il y'avait beaucoup d'autres personnes dans le cinéma?*" ("Were there many other people in the cinema?") to which I responded: "*Oui, il y'avait beaucoup de vieux hommes qui faisent ca*" ("Yes, there were lots of old men who did this") and I simulated a man wanking (though I really didn't understand what I was doing). Sylvie's mother looked absolutely shocked and started to question me about where the men were so then I said that I was joking. She seemed very quiet after that and I realised that I'd done something wrong and that it must have been due to my "joke" but I still didn't really understand why it had shocked her so much. Sylvie wasn't quite so friendly with me for a while after that and I wasn't invited to her house for some weeks.

'I go back to going to see Joss each weekend and, near the Easter holidays she casually mentions: "We won't be here after Easter because we are moving to the south of France." I am stunned and say nothing but when I returned to Fabienne's I phone my mum crying, saying: "I couldn't manage to stay without them because the weekends are so long." I then run into Fabienne's bedroom and lie on her bed crying. My father marches into the bedroom and shouts at me: "What are you thinking of, phoning your mother and upsetting her?" I can't find any words to say to him and sit on the side of the bed silently crying. Fabienne comes in and asks me why it will be so bad and I can't really explain so they both leave me alone in her bedroom.'

I shouted in an exasperated voice towards Vida: 'He never stopped ignoring my pain; everybody else was more important than me and Ray.'

Vida was nodding. 'Yes, that's true.' I was immersed in making sure my kind therapist heard the details of this time in my life.

'As the holidays approach Joss asks if I would like to spend them with her and Philippe in their new home. It saves me from having to go back to England and we travel down in a car full of their belongings and, when we arrive, are shown to a large upstairs flat. We arrive on a Friday evening and Philippe has the weekend free so on Saturday evening we go to a restaurant and then the cinema. We go to see *Petit Grand Homme* (Little Big Man) with the lead man played by Dustin Hoffman. The story is about how the white settlers oppressed and killed the American Indians. I am fully involved in the story and, when the soldiers kill the American Indian babies and young children, I have to stifle a huge, body-aching sob; I can't fathom how any human could ever harm any baby or young child. I am quiet for a while after and feel deeply, desperately hopeless at the mere thought that babies and young children might be harmed deliberately by grown-up people but I can't articulate my feelings clearly either to myself or to Joss.

'About ten days into my visit, while out walking with Joss in a secluded forest, we pass a young man on his own and he stops to have a chat but as we start to leave he grabs my arm and says something like: "*Tu viens avec moi?*" ("Will you come with me?"), I pull away speechless with fear and shock. He lunges at me again but Joss does nothing because she seems paralysed and is just staring at us. The tussle seems to go on and on with him pushing me away from Joss. Then, at last, Joss walks towards us and grabs his arm and says very quietly: "*Laisse l'a tranquille*" ("Leave her alone"). He tries to push her away but she persists and finally he gives up and walks quickly away from us. We stand, stunned into silence, watching him recede into the distance, then walk briskly (Joss won't run) back to the car. Joss drives us back to the flat in silence and doesn't tell Philippe or ever talk about it again and I understand that, for some reason, she absolutely doesn't want to discuss it.

'The atmosphere between us has changed and I'm very happy to return to Paris. Fabienne makes her usual big fuss of me when I arrive but this time I don't enjoy it. My father is not there because his sabbatical has finished and he's now back living in England. I feel heavy and strange and miss my mum so I write to her to ask her for a photo because I don't have one of her. I guess the events of the holiday have frightened me.

'I go back to school for my last term and Sylvie becomes a close friend again but she only takes me to her flat when her mother isn't around. My problems with relationships suddenly get much worse because Fabienne goes away for a weekend with Cecile to visit friends, leaving me to be cared for by Charles and a female cousin of hers in her early twenties. She casually asks me how had I met Louis and I, surprised that Fabienne hadn't told her, say: "*Mais il est mon pere*" ("But he is my father"). She looks very shocked and asks me all about my family, to which I respond openly, not suspecting that there is anything wrong in what I tell her; nobody has said that I need to be secretive with Fabienne's family and, after all, I reason that Cecile is also illegitimate.

'The next thing I hear is Charles shouting at the cousin in his bedroom and then rushing into the living room, shouting angrily at me: "*Tu sais que je ne veux pas que to reste dans cette maison*" ("You know that I don't want you to stay in this house any more"). I am utterly shocked and reply: "*Pourquoi?*" ("Why?")to which he responds by turning, marching out of the room, grabbing his coat and storming out of the flat. The cousin comes back into the living room and tries to pass it off by explaining that he's got a bad temper but it'll blow over and won't tell me why he's so angry with me. The next day, Fabienne arrives back with Cecile and the first thing I hear is her and Charles having a huge argument in his bedroom (he hasn't come out of his room since he returned to the flat the previous evening). Fabienne then comes to me, after having a quiet talk with her cousin, echoing the cousin's words telling me: "*Il a de mauvais humeur*" ("He's got a bad temper") and "*ca va passer*" ("it'll blow over") but won't tell me what I've done wrong.'

'I am completely confused and don't have any idea what I have done wrong. It didn't occur to me till I was much older that Charles hadn't known that I was my father's daughter. How could my father and Fabienne put me in that position?' My words bounced loudly around the room. I looked straight at Vida and continued.

'His anger towards me doesn't blow over and he completely ignores me for the rest of my stay and Fabienne and my father don't do anything to try to stop his behaviour towards me (a child of fourteen years). I don't bother to tell my mother because I am fearful of my father's reaction but I do spend more and more time with Sylvie and she manages to get her mother to allow me back to her flat so I start to stay with her at the weekends.

'I then have an argument with Fabienne because my father arrives late one night en route to some conference and they are talking very loudly in the kitchen. The living room is directly next door and the noise they are making is stopping me from sleeping and I bang on the wall to let them know. Fabienne storms into the living room shouting furiously: "*Ca suffi et tu dois etre plus poli et venire dire bonjour a ton pere*" ("That's enough and you should be more polite and go to say hello to your father").

'I lie in bed hurt and bereft and my father doesn't bother to come to see me and he leaves early next morning without saying either "hello" or "goodbye". I return from school that evening and

Cecile is at home with her nanny. Her nanny is an elderly woman who I have tried to avoid because I find her creepy but to day she asks me: "*Tu est triste, quesqu'il ya?*" ("You are sad, what's wrong?"). I mumble something about Fabienne being cross with me and she tells me that Fabienne gets cross easily and goes and makes me some hot chocolate.

'That evening I can't speak to Fabienne and she ignores me. By 9 p.m. she asks me if I have eaten and makes me dinner and things seem back to "normal" but we never talk about why she was so angry with me. I am not quite as enthusiastic about Fabienne after this and start to spend time with the nanny and Cecile. On Wednesdays (French schools have Wednesdays off and we go in on Saturday mornings) instead of going to Sylvie's I now go to the park with Cecile and her nanny and then we go back to her flat for "*goûter*" (tea).'

I was slightly calmer. 'I think she provided me with much-needed warmth that had vanished from Charles and Fabienne and sustained me for those last few weeks.' My warm Vida looked towards me with her achingly beautiful eyes.

'You were in the middle of events that were not in any way caused by you. The adults around you were very absorbed in their own lives and let you down badly.'

'You're too fucking right and it didn't get any better.' I replied with angry hopelessness.

'My father visits for a weekend and enters the flat with presents for Fabienne (a pearl necklace) and Cecile (a toy) and, after all the giving and hugging, turns to me and merely says: "Hello." I can't understand why he does this and the humiliation of this event is deep. Then Joss and Philippe return and are invited to dinner by Fabienne and my father, and Charles makes a point of making a huge fuss of Joss while obviously ignoring me and Joss looks across at me smiling with what looks like triumphant glee. Why? I don't understand even now, except perhaps my sister really disliked me much more than she ever liked me.

'The day of my departure arrives and Fabienne has left for work without saying goodbye. Cecile's nanny has brought a huge box of chocolates for me, which I have never had before. I am deeply touched. She embraces me and I leave with my rucksack and walk to the underground to make my own way back to my mother's house. I am sitting on the underground and catch my face in the window and the tears begin to roll silently down my face and I struggle to stop them flowing.

'I arrive "home" and soon after start my new school. This is because the French summer term ends about two weeks before the English school term. Although there is no uniform, girls have to wear skirts and my mother has applied for a clothes allowance (she is on benefits) to pay for my school clothes. The clothes have to be bought from the Co-op and the assistants look at us with pity when we hand over our coupon; such a contrast from Fabienne, who took me to Parisian boutiques. My mother doesn't seem aware of the humiliation factor and actually seems to be enjoying the pitying attention. She plays the role of "ill mother" very well, groaning loudly as she sat down on a requested seat because her back is in "spasm". It is excruciatingly embarrassing, especially because her groans sound the same as when Joss is having sex. We return "home" and, thankfully, I now have my own room with Joss's old record player and play Joss's Beatles records endlessly. Some of their songs make me cry, particularly "Blackbird," "Yesterday" and "Eleanor Rigby".'

I heard gentle, distant words floating towards me: 'Your time in France had been another very difficult time in your life.' A deeply sad silence filled the room. I drove home feeling like shit.

Chapter 8

I passed my diploma with a distinction and my thoughts were turning to trying to get a part-time counselling job. The problem with my course was that it was mainly theoretical (we had very few practice sessions) so getting a post in counselling was virtually impossible; if I wanted to pursue counselling I would have to either do another course or become a volunteer counsellor. I felt that I was obliged to start earning some money and got a part-time job as a 'welfare advisor' in a student advice centre (though I would have preferred to try to become a registered counsellor). Despite my reservations I was quite surprised that I'd been offered a job and was excitedly telling Vida.

'They've offered me the job. The only problem is that it's a fixed contract (one year) and they can't say whether they'll have the money to renew.'

It was unusual for me to be animated with good news for my patient doctor and she beamed her widest smile at me.

'Congratulations. You've done very well with your diploma and now getting this job. When do you start?'

'In three weeks and I'm very nervous; how will I manage to talk to all the different people?' I felt sick as I told Vida my fears.

'Well, it's normal for people to be nervous when they start new things and I'm sure your new work colleagues will help you,' Vida said, trying to reassure me.

'Yes, but what if I can't stop blushing? You know I blush so easily and it's so embarrassing because I go so red it's impossible to ignore it.' I blushed puce red while speaking because I found even talking about my blushing problem embarrassing. Vida talked to me in her calmest voice.

'I'm sure that as you settle down you will get less anxious.' I felt that she didn't really understand how bad my symptoms were so I retreated into a silence unsure of how I would really cope with my new job. The weeks up to my new job passed very quickly and I was soon into my new routine of work, looking after the children, housework and shopping (Simon was very busy in his job trying to make sure they would renew his contract) which didn't leave much time for anything else. I had started in the summer holidays so I didn't see any students and my role was to network with other welfare services, produce publicity materials and organise a series of talks for the first year students at the beginning of the autumn term.

I was coping quite well with the networking (even with the occasional bright red blush) when, at the end of a meeting I'd had with a male colleague (I had felt very uncomfortable by the way he looked at me), he tried to kiss me. I managed to turn my head so he only kissed my cheek but it left me shaken. I didn't know what to do and at my next session with Vida, told her.

'What can I do about this horrible man who I'm supposed to work with? He won't stop looking at me in a horrible way and he tried to kiss me.'

'What do you mean "in a horrible way"?'

'You know, like pervy leering.' I blushed red as I said these words because I found it so awkward.

'You must go and get advice from a trusted colleague and make sure the person has it on record that the man has tried to kiss you; it is not acceptable behaviour and there are sexual harassment laws.'

'Do you think I did anything to make him do that?'

'I doubt it. I'm afraid that with male colleagues like that you just have to be extremely careful with your boundaries by keeping any conversations to work agendas.'

Her words had given me confidence in my right to stand up to this man. 'I do have a friendly woman colleague who I could tell and I'll not discuss anything with him except work.'

At work, I sent an email to my friend (so it was on record) explaining the kissing incident. She replied in a flippant tone with the closing words: 'It's never happened to me.' This made me feel a bit ridiculous but I focussed on what Vida had said to me and distanced myself from my new friend. I was also very careful when in proximity to the man, making sure I never smiled at him, and it seemed to work because he stopped bothering me. I began to feel better than I had for ages and was enjoying being at work because I'd begun to make friends, meeting them for coffee and lunches. I still socialised very little outside of work but I was hopeful that as I got to know my new work friends this might change. However, as the autumn approached I started to become very anxious about the talk I would have to give to about two hundred new students. I sat with Vida, trying to explain to her my extreme fear and began remembering my first experience of giving a talk when at poly in my first year.

'Part of our coursework involves giving talks to the other students and lecturers and I find the idea of being the sole focus of a group very frightening though all I am aware of is a growing feeling (as the talk approaches) of hopelessness and despondency. It gets so bad that suicidal thoughts flash through my mind. This means that I find it very difficult to actually prepare my talk. I leave it until as late as possible and only practice a couple of times. I can't even bear to practice in front of Simon but I do force myself to attend the seminar and do my talk. Although I manage to give my seminar, done very fast and with a red face, when it comes to the questions, I start well by answering a couple, but then I am asked a question I can't answer. Instead of simply saying: "I don't know", I freeze and stare out of the window and say absolutely nothing. I feel so far away from the room and people that I am unable to speak; I have been catapulted into another realm which traps me in a floaty and opaque world yet my body is still in the lecture room.

'The whole room becomes drenched in an awkward silence and the lecturer takes what seems like an age to realise that I'm not going to answer and finally, in an embarrassed way, thanks me for my talk and the room rapidly bursts into a relieved loud clap. We then have a coffee break and many of the other students look at me in a pitying way (which I really hate) and even Simon looks a bit uncomfortable. I don't even discuss it with Simon later and I do my best to forget about my strange uncontrollable behaviour in front of all those people. I manage to only do one more seminar on this course, which I also mess up.

During my PhD, again I am faced with the dreaded seminars.

I have to present a talk to about two hundred people about my work and produce a poster for a stand and be present to explain my work. I practice my talk endlessly and when the time comes to do it I know it so well by heart that I simply 'switch off' and say the words. But then there are questions and my brain is not working properly and, when I can't answer a particular question, I freeze solid and my mouth won't move. The whole room full of people sit tensely, staring at me, waiting for me to say something; it seems to go on and on and finally a lecturer says something and a discussion follows and no one asks me any more questions. I do tentatively ask my supervisor about nerves in public speaking but he dismissively says: "We all have them and they go away eventually", but I have not seen anybody else freeze like I did and, as similar events happened to me during my degree, I feel it is uncontrollable and from then on I avoid all situations of public speaking.'

'When I started my PhD I thought I could overcome my nerves by being very well prepared but that didn't work so what can I do?' I asked Vida desperately. Vida looked towards me bored.

'Well, if you don't know the answer to a question simply say you don't know and move on.'

I felt I was losing Vida's attention and, endeavouring to sound reassured, replied: 'Yes, I'll just do that and I'm sure it'll be fine.'

I didn't discuss these fears with her again until having attempted to give my talk. I was sitting despondently in front of Vida, telling her of my failure.

'I gave my talk but it was awful because I talked like a robot, got my slides mixed up and I could see embarrassed looks on my colleagues faces and I've been off sick since.' Vida looked at me uncomprehendingly.

'If it was that bad I'm not surprised you're ill. Haven't you got any work colleagues who can help and support you?'

'Well, Simon does let me practice my talk with him so I suppose next time I could just practice more.'

We didn't discuss this again and my job began to slide into a place of me trying to avoid any public speaking and to be as bright and bubbly as possible with work colleagues. I kept thinking my job would get better as I got more confidence and, now that I had a reasonably 'normal' life, I set a date with Vida for our last session. The date was set for three weeks before my fortieth birthday; I would have been in therapy for five and a half years (I considered that this should definitely have been enough). In the second to last session, I couldn't think of anything to say to her so I burst out: 'Well, I seem to have run out of things to say to you so I think we should end it now.' Vida shifted awkwardly in her chair.

'Well, if that's what you feel you want to do then so be it.'

'Thank you for all your help.'

'You have worked very hard at your therapy and I wish you well in the future.' I got up stiffly to leave and, just as I was about to go through the door, I turned to her, holding out my hand.

'I've never touched you.'

She looked embarrassed but shook my hand and I was surprised because hers was hot and damp. I walked quickly from the building, tears threatening to overwhelm me. I got to my car and sobbed (this was very unusual for me). I felt very odd for the next few weeks, occasionally bursting into tears (only when alone). My fortieth birthday was disappointing (I had no party and didn't see any of my few friends). My children and Simon tried hard to make my birthday happy. Their attention and presents gave me some warmth and joy yet underneath I felt desperately depressed and empty. I wished I was dead and felt very guilty towards my children for having these feelings. My work was awful (I wouldn't admit it) and I became very thin and exhausted. Most mornings I felt so dizzy I could hardly stand but I kept thinking things would get better. After all, I'd had five and a half years of therapy.

Then I was told that Simon's contract was not to be renewed and, soon after, neither was mine. It was three months since I'd left therapy and I was desperate so I wrote to Vida asking to see her again; she gave me an appointment two months later. I was suddenly back, sitting facing the warm enigma of my therapist.

'I can't understand why we haven't got our contracts renewed. We've worked so hard! I can't face going back on the dole. We might loose our house. What are we doing wrong?'

108

'Well, are you both applying for other jobs?'

'Simon has decided to put all his efforts into his consultancy and I thought that I would do a bereavement counselling course with a view to developing my career in counselling.' I was trying to sound confident. Vida smiled.

'So you have both thought about how you are going to deal with the loss of your jobs?' I shifted awkwardly.

'Yes, but I'm worried about whether Simon will actually earn any money and my plan doesn't involve earnings for at least a year, until I have enough practice hours to apply for jobs. I'm exhausted and I need to get a job with long-term stability and I think my only option is to try for counselling though I'm worried about not earning.'

'Well, you do look very tired so maybe some time to think about your next moves would be good.'

Vida's words echoed my feelings of being in desperate need of some respite from trying to work in a job that made me ill. I lifted my heavy head towards those familiar yet strange brown eyes.

'Can I come to see you weekly until I've sorted my job problems out?' A long, tight silence ensued before Vida shifted forcefully in her seat.

'Yes, that should be OK. We'll try it and see how it goes.' I didn't feel welcomed by her words; I detected some reluctance but was so pleased to have her help again that I left this session in a bubble of relief.

I left my job, with no send-off (I did get a couple of cards), yet I missed talking to my colleagues. I was back at home, again, not having made any friends at my job and was just managing to see a couple of women friends every few weeks; occasionally, we had a dinner party with one of my friends and her husband. I was convinced that once my career as a counsellor began that I would be freed from my exhausting (often suicidal) depressions.

I arrived nervously at the first session of my bereavement counselling course and was pleased to find a couple of students from my diploma had also enrolled. The facilitators gave an introduction, emphasising that they sometimes found that people came to the course because they hadn't adequately grieved their own bereavements and that we should let them know if we thought this might become a problem (I didn't really understand what they meant because I had little idea of the grieving process). I began to enjoy the weekly practice sessions and really felt that I might, at last, be on the right career path, particularly as one of the facilitators said to me: 'You are incredibly good at this. I've never seen such a sensitive student.'

However, a few weeks into the course, a group activity was set where we had to share our own experiences of death of a loved one and, when it came to my turn, I began to tell them of the death of my pet gerbil. I could hear myself talking but was feeling completely numb when suddenly my voice changed and I turned to the group and said: 'I'm avoiding telling you about my abortion when I was fifteen years old and my father's suicide when I was twenty-nine years old.'

The group leader then responded rapidly. 'I'm so glad you've shared your abortion with us because this has never come up before and we need to deal with grief associated with abortions. In fact, I had one as a teenager and have never shared it with the other counsellors.'

I drove home with persistent thoughts of my abortion and at my next session with Vida I revisited the time when Joss had her first baby.

'In my first flat, my father visits me every few weeks and, on one of his first visits, he tells me in an exuberant voice that Joss is pregnant. He doesn't consider that I might be sensitive to this (it's almost exactly a year since I had my abortion) and all I can remember is my physical surroundings; the room we are in, the way my father is standing with his hands in the pockets of his long winter coat. A few weeks later, I go to stay with Joss and say to her: "You do realise that you are doing exactly what I want to do? I would love to have a baby."

'She replies with a triumphant smile that I can still see so clearly: "I know."

'I then suggest: "You could have had my baby."

'"It would never have worked because you would never have stopped wanting to look after it yourself and it would never have been really mine," she replied. When her son, Marcel (Marc) is born, I can't wait to see him and when I first see him in the hospital cot I gently stroke his beautiful cheek, feeling overwhelmed with love for him.

'Joss comes home a few days later and stays with my mother for a couple of weeks. I visit as often as possible because I adore Marc and love holding him, especially when he falls asleep in my arms. Joss and Philippe aren't very good with him and I am aghast when Marc is shrieking and Philippe jiggles him roughly up and down so that his head wobbles uncomfortably. I am surprised that Joss says nothing and leaves Philippe trying to calm Marc in such an insensitive way. I long to say something but don't dare. Joss seems awkward and distant with him and she gets cross with me when she enters the room seeing Marc comfortably asleep on my shoulder and she grabs him roughly off me. They leave when Marc is about two weeks old and I do miss him, though I am glad to be away from Joss's anger.'

I looked at Vida. 'I was obviously feeling the loss of my baby without realising it and maybe Joss was enjoying seeing me suffer. Did she have her baby in response to my pregnancy? Were the pregnancies linked? I feel that they were but then I think I must be mistaken. She can't have hated me that much, or maybe the truth is too hurtful. At the time I didn't consciously think about it but now I feel that they somehow stole my baby from me and I know it's irrational.' I turned to stare at my tree with its brown, fading leaves and I was soon disturbed by some soft words piercing my blissful floating.

'Yes, I think it's possible that your pregnancies were linked in some way, as envy between you was not managed well by your parents when you were small children.' Her comments propelled me forwards to my own pregnancy with my daughter.

'When I am only a few weeks into my pregnancy with Sophie, Joss phones me and says aggressively: "So when's this baby going to be born?" Then, when I am about four months pregnant, I am staying with her and we are all having a meal at my mother's and she gives a sealed card to her eldest child, Marc. He's confused as it isn't his birthday and Joss explains that it's some good news for all of them. Marc opens the card slowly and we can see a picture of a teddy bear and, as he opens it, he reads out: "You are going to have a new baby brother or sister." Silence fills the room and we turn to Joss asking when. She has an odd triumphant expression when saying: "A few weeks after Aunty Marian's baby is to be born.""

I looked at Vida, confused. 'Do you think she subconsciously chose to have her fourth child at the same time as mine because it felt like she couldn't bear me to be the centre of attention?'

'Well, yes, it is possible that her envy of you would drive her to extreme lengths.' Vida looked towards me clearly and pushed my thoughts on.

'Whenever I'm with her she can be very off-hand and insensitive with Sophie. It's almost as if she treats her with the same irritation as me. Her daughters also sometimes treat Sophie so horribly that I have to intervene and Joss rarely says anything about her children's behaviour towards Sophie.'

'Family patterns can carry on through generations and it's important to try to address the issues leading to the negative behaviours so it can stop.' I left this session feeling that I had to try harder to stop Joss and her daughters being horrible to Sophie because there were times when I didn't say anything (I was frightened of Joss's anger).

I was soon given an opportunity to challenge my sister's attitude towards me as Christmas was imminent. Joss took Christmas very seriously and would spend ages organising the stockings for her children and also took care in presents for my mother, me and my family and this year was no exception. I received three wrapped presents for Simon, Sophie and Adrian and an envelope for me. I still felt upset towards Joss because of the resurrection of issues around my abortion so I was quite sensitive and felt aggrieved that I didn't have a wrapped present like the rest of my family.

I put aside the presents for my children and, with Simon, opened his present and my envelope. Simon had a pair of warm gloves and I had a voucher for two cinema tickets; I felt I'd been treated unfairly and Joss had often behaved slightly oddly around

Simon. Simon was adamant he hated the gloves and I decided to send them back to her explaining that, although we appreciated the thought, Simon didn't need them because he had loads of pairs of gloves. About ten days later, I got a phone call from my mother telling me how much I had upset Joss and asking me why I would think of sending a present back. My mother kept repeating: 'It's not the done thing, you know.' I said as little as possible to her, fearing a usual response of ridicule.

A few days after Christmas, I received a two-page letter from Joss telling me, in a very angry, patronising and condescending way, that she would never speak me, my children or Simon again (I knew she meant it because, after her marriage broke up, she literally didn't speak to her ex-husband for years). I ran to my next session with Vida bursting to tell her what had happened.

'Joss has sent me the most horrible letter and it proves that she never cared about my children because she has said that she'll never speak to them, as well. I feel like she's beaten me up and I feel pain in my tummy.' Vida looked very surprised and took a few minutes to reply.

'Well she has, in a way, beaten you up and, now you know the truth, maybe it's time to let her go.'

'Yes, but how could she do that to my children? I can understand her being upset towards me but to be so extreme in her reaction! What do I say to Sophie and Adrian? Adrian and her youngest son really like each other.'

'You will simply have to explain to them that you've had a disagreement with your sister, that is nothing to do with them, but that it means you need some time apart and that they won't be able to see their cousins for a while,' my calm, brown-eyed friend said reassuringly. I started to see some advantages to my separation from my sister.

'I suppose I'm released from ever having to suffer her off-hand, angry comments again and I guess Sophie will also be free from her put-downs.'

'Yes. Sometimes letting go is the better solution and you don't know what may happen in the future.' Vida looked down at her wrist with the usual: 'Shall we continue next week?'

I hardly had any time to think before I was back in my

bereavement course, listening to a session on the particular difficulties in dealing with death through suicide. I sat feeling very awkward as thoughts tumbled through my mind about my father's suicide. The next days at home I was looking through photographs of my father and reading letters and cards he had sent to me since I was a small child at Summerhill. I couldn't understand what I meant to him and, at my session with Vida, remembered my times with him.

'I am about eight years old and my father meets us from the train in Paris. We have a few hours to spare so he takes us to the Eiffel Tower. We have been a few times because whenever we have had time in Paris he has taken us to see it. He absolutely loves it and becomes animated whenever we approach. He likes to park a few streets away so, as we walk towards it, along the wide avenues lined with trees and fountains, he can spend the time describing how it was built and how it's so amazing that few people thought it was anything special and there were even serious objections to its construction. Then he always says triumphantly: "Look, it's a central attraction in Paris now, Paris is the *Tour Eiffel*." I really enjoy my father's enthusiasm and do appreciate the tower's beauty and the wonderful views from the top. We either walk up or take the lift, depending on whether Ray or I win the argument, because I prefer the lift (the steps were quite scary) and Ray prefers the excitement of the stairs.

'During this year, my father comes to visit us at Summerhill with a French lady, not his wife, but as I learn later, a new French lover of his called Fabienne. She seems very interested in us but can hardly speak English. As he is leaving I have an overwhelming feeling of sadness and desperation and chase after his car sobbing, but he continued to wave out of the car window and doesn't notice my distress. I stand at the gates crying for a long time not really knowing why.'

I sat hunched in my chair gazing at some mark on her carpet while Vida's warm silence covered me with cotton wool. I then lifted my eyes to hers. 'How can I be still going over what happened with my father. Why isn't it out of my head?'

'Maybe you haven't fully grieved his death yet,' Vida suggests.

'I hadn't thought of that, but why does it take so long?' I then move quickly into another memory.

'I am twenty-three years old and am going to France because my father has invited me to go on holiday with him and Cecile. I go to stay with Fabienne and Cecile (I can't stay at my father's because he is with his wife) for a few days before we go on holiday. It's the first time I've stayed with Fabienne since I lived with her when I was thirteen years old. The morning that we are leaving Fabienne says to me: "*C'est la premiere fois que tu est allée en vacances avec ton pere?*" ("Is it the first time you've ever been on holiday with your father?")

'"Oui" I reply.

'This thought goes around in my head for the rest of my holiday and makes me feel alone and confused. We go to the Alps and I am filled with a joy that I haven't often experienced because I absolutely love the awesome beauty of the mountains. My father seems slightly vacant and seems to have trouble with his co-ordination and I query whether he's fine but he just laughs my concerns away. The holiday is quite strained as I feel tense and uncomfortable with my father; so many of my thoughts are left unsaid to him.

'We return to Paris and, a few days later, my father asks me out for the day and apologises to me, in a flippant way, for my childhood. After I return to England, my lack of response to my father's apology was nagging at me so I write him a long letter explaining my feelings towards him but before I get to send it I am on the phone to him and he tells me he's been diagnosed with Parkinson's disease. I never send him the letter, feeling that I can't confront him now that he is ill, and I try to get on with my life. Soon after this, I spend some time with my father alone visiting Paris and, because of his recent diagnosis, he seems to want to talk about death and his will. I can't quite remember how he puts it but it becomes clear that his "legitimate" children stand to inherit a much larger portion of his estate than us (his "illegitimate" children). He explains that it is like this because of French law and that he can do nothing; I am enraged and say if I'm not to be equal to his "legitimate" children, I want nothing. This really upsets him and he remains silent for most of the rest of my visit.'

I turned angrily to Vida. 'He wasn't as helpless as he made us believe because he had a flat in London, and two flats in Paris so he could easily have sold one and given us our rightful share himself. But he never saw us as equivalent. He said to my mother when we were young children: "My wife and children must never suffer because of you and your children." My mother said nothing in our defence. He died not having put it right because his estate was worth about three quarters of a million pounds yet we (myself and my illegitimate brother and sisters) got £7,500 each and my mother got nothing. We only got the £7,500 because I had insisted, when I was eighteen years old, that he give me some sort of proof that he was my father (he signed an affidavit) so we would have got nothing if I hadn't had the legal proof.'

I sat crumpled in my chair, feeling that the truth was that my father didn't really love me. Those warm, brown eyes looked deeply at me.

'I think it's true that his attitude towards you didn't change much during his life and that, clearly, you were treated very unfairly.' I left this session feeling the full force of the fact that my father never saw me as anything but one of his illegitimate children and that we were somehow considered to have fewer needs than his legitimate offspring. My thoughts were a whirl of memories of my father and in my next therapy session I was very surprised by the words that seem to come involuntarily from my mouth.

'My father chucked himself into a river in the middle of the night. I can't bear to think of the pain he must have suffered. Imagine going into a cold river knowing that you can't swim because of your illness and drowning. Imagine the slow, painful, lonely walk (he could hardly walk without help) from his flat down to the cold, dark river.

'How could he have done that to himself?' I asked pleadingly of my soft, warm, friendly doctor. 'You loved your father?' Vida's last words echoed round my mind and I responded with a sob.

'Yes, I must have, but he didn't love me!' I swallowed my crying and moved on to his funeral.

'It is a Sunday (it's funny how memories seem to emphasise seemingly insignificant details, and I definitely remember it was a Sunday because I'd just cooked a roast chicken). The phone rings and Simon answers it. He seems to chat for a while and then says very quietly to me: "Your sister has something to tell you" and I feel a bit odd and carefully put the phone to my ear. My sister says in a dead, flat tone: "Louis is dead." I throw the phone out of my hand as I scream and run upstairs to my bed where I hug myself and roll from side to side screaming.'

I couldn't stop the tears rolling down my face as I said: 'I don't understand why I reacted like that. After all, I'd hardly seen him for the last two years of his life.' I moved on with my memories of that day.

'Simon comes up looking at me in a pained, pitying way and Sophie comes up behind, which brings me to my senses. I stop immediately, saying to her: "Don't worry, darling. Mummy's just had a shock because her daddy has died" (Sophie has only met him a couple of times so didn't really know him as her granddad). I cry on and off for about twenty-four hours and then I begin to feel very strangely elated; I suddenly feel it is over, my painful relationship with my father is finished and I feel free.

'Mind you, that feeling didn't last and here I am, ten years later, still trying to understand my relationship with my father.' I said in an exasperated way to Vida.

'Well, it was a very painful relationship for you and it takes time to process those painful feelings.' Her soft tones gently remind me of my hurt.

'You mean because he's dead there is no possibility that the relationship will get any better so I have to accept it the way it was.'

'Yes, that's exactly how it is.' My doctor's voice was emphatic. I began to laugh.

'The funeral is like a comedy show; we go to the funeral place to see his body and my sister won't come, saying adamantly: "I want to remember him how he was", so after the legitimate family have viewed him I go in with my brother. He takes one look at my father's body and runs out. I stand alone, staring at my father's impassive, yet empty face and I really feel that he has gone. His body literally looks like an empty case, which gives me a feeling of surprise and relief. I am desperate to touch him; I want to physically feel his skin beneath my hand and, I look back to see if anyone is there, then lean forward and quickly touch his forehead with my right fingers. I sort of press my fingers into his forehead and it is like concrete; the softness of a live body is gone. I wish I could have stroked his face but I am frightened that someone might see me.

'We then drive to the church, his coffin in a grey-coloured van similar to those used by market stallholders and builders (I am surprised, but nobody questions it). His legitimate daughter and wife sit in the front (we are not assigned an official car). At the church, the priest begins his speech and, at the end, asks that the family of the deceased stand. I start to move up from my seat and turn towards my sister who isn't moving so I sit back down, feeling angry with her for being so pathetic and angry with myself for not having the courage to stand alone. Then there is an amazingly beautiful voice of a woman singing slow, deeply touching notes, which is a surprise to me and makes me cry. At the graveside two old friends of his give speeches, mentioning his wife and three children, but not my mother or us.'

I rejoined Vida. 'Yes, you are right. Even at his funeral we were expected to remain as "friends of the family". Nothing ever changed. I sometimes wish that I'd never gone to his funeral but I am glad I saw his body.'

'Yes, it does help to face the reality of a death when seeing the body.' Vida commented. Another fifty minutes with my replacement mum (as I often jokingly referred to her with Simon) was over and I had to leave.

Over the following weeks, I kept looking through my childhood photographs, trying to understand why my father even bothered to see us. One day I happened to be talking on the phone to my mother and I began asking about my early childhood, trying to find out why my father never left his wife for my mother. The conversation ambled along, not really going anywhere, and somehow I turned to the foster homes we'd stayed in and was told that I'd been with one carer much longer than I'd ever known. I charged into my next meeting with Vida and breathlessly told her.

'I was trying to ascertain a chronological picture of my early child-care by asking my mother the order of care. I had assumed that had stayed at "the policeman's" for only a weekend yet my mother casually told me: "Of course, you were there for three to four months." My mother then added in an exuberant, triumphant voice: "Ha, the Social Services had to care for you as I was ill" (she had often phoned the Social Services to ask them to look after us when she was "desperate" and they had refused).

'My body had reacted violently to this information by slumping forward as if severely winded and by my involuntarily yelling: "Not three months" without knowing why.

'Then she casually told me: "Your father took you to and from the foster carers and nursery, so you did see him nearly every day." I was swirling in confusion when she then told me that Joss had stayed with Robert, and visited my mother with him but my brother and I didn't see her for the whole period. I asked her if she had tried to get to see us and she replied gruffly: "Oh well, I did need a rest. After all, I had had the most dreadful year."'

I sat shaking. 'How could my father have done that to us, to take me and Ray to and from foster care and then go home to his wife and daughter and not take us with him? How could he have done that to us and to have never have talked to me about it when I was older? I was four and a half years old, my brother even younger. How could my father have not wanted to care for us himself?' Vida looked directly at me.

'You've had a shock finding out about this time in your life and again your father caused you considerable pain.'

'It's not just that. There's more,' I gasp.

'It began on a Sunday, so my mother tells me, she is very specific about the fact it was a Sunday, she woke up with a ghastly pain in her upper abdomen, a very sharp piercing pain that was so bad she was doubled up and crying and yelling.

'She screams for Joss to phone for the doctor. He arrives and thinks that my mother is mentally ill with hysteria and has her sectioned and admitted to the local mental hospital. We, my brother and I, are taken into emergency foster care for three to four months (my mother can't quite remember the exact time but it was from about September to early January) by the Social Services and placed with a retired policemen and his wife who had been a nurse. It gets worse as my mother describes to me how nice it is when she leaves hospital a week or so before Christmas and is just with Joss. "You know what it's like when you only have one child. Suddenly you can do things again. I remember painting a cupboard with Joss." Just when I think it can't get any more devastating, she tells me that it isn't that bad because before she went to her aunt's for Christmas with Joss, she dropped off some presents for Ray and me at the foster home. "So you got what you usually did. It was only an extra week or so" were her final words on the subject to me.'

I was frantic. 'How could my mother do that to me? After all that time she casually "popped in" to see us and left us again, at Christmas. And my father went, as usual to France. Why didn't he look after my mum? She was ill! We were so little and neither of my parents would look after us. I hate them both and I know they both didn't love me.'

My soft, warm mum-replacement calmly told me: 'Your parents were certainly very neglectful of yours and your brother's needs and your mother still doesn't seem to understand the significance of her behaviour towards you.'

I was caught up in thoughts of the foster care. 'It's strange because I had no conscious memories of this episode in foster care, yet I have such clear memories preceding this event and I keep hearing a voice, that I think is the policeman, saying: "These ones are not to be marked." What could that mean?' I looked towards Vida in confusion and she spoke seriously.

'It is a shock to you to have found out about this foster home and maybe more memories of this time will come back to you.'

'I have a horrible feeling about that place and why would I, because the woman teacher I stayed with a few months before I remember and I really liked her? I just can't understand any of it and how could my mother and father have done that to me?' Vida smiled at me while trying to look at her watch, reminding me of time.

I left the session feeling odd and, when I got to the car park, I couldn't remember where my car was or, more disturbingly, what it looked like. I stood in the middle of the car park feeling very panicky and had to concentrate very hard to try to get a picture of my car; my mind went back to my father's car. It must have been the one in which he drove us to and from the foster home. It still had the plastic on the seats because he didn't want the car to get dirty. It was blue. I then tried to focus on my surroundings and get a picture of my previous car, which was blue, and I started to walk around looking for it, then I suddenly saw a familiar maroon car and remembered that it was mine. I couldn't understand what was happening to me and felt very weird and floaty for the next few weeks, though I managed to carry on with my counselling course and caring for my children.

At a later meeting with Vida, I told her about my car park incident (which had happened again) and then went on to ask her: 'Why do I keep getting a voice in my head saying "they are not to be marked"?' Vida shifted in her chair and looked directly at me with her most serious face.

'Well, I don't know. What do you think it means?'

I stared at the newly opened, bright, green leaves of my comforting tree as it brushed against the windowpane. I then abruptly told her: 'You know, I've started to get other voices in my head which say really horrible things about a person I happen to be speaking to.'

'What horrible things do the voices say?' asked Vida in a very matter-of-fact tone.

'Oh, you know, about the way they look and sometimes sort of about sex. It's really yucky.' I looked at the ground while speaking.

'When does this happen to you?' my calming doctor asked.

'Well, I've never told anybody but the first time I remember it happening was when I was working, soon after my Dad died, and I was talking to another member of staff. A voice in my head said some terrible things about her and all I could do was sort of freeze and try to get away from her as fast as possible. I left this job soon after and I don't really remember it happening much again until now and it's nearly every day when I'm in shops and occasionally when I'm talking to Simon, which I find really disturbing.'

I omitted to tell Vida that it also happened with her and that a voice in my head would say: 'You're a stupid, ugly bitch and what do you think your fat, ugly therapist will do for you? Ha, ha, ha.' The laughing was bouncing very, very loudly around my head and I wanted to cover my ears and put my head on my knees but I knew it wouldn't do any good. I just couldn't get away from the voices in my head and I was very scared. I turned desperately to Vida.

'Am I going fucking mad?'

Vida seemed completely undisturbed by my revelations and firmly told me: 'No, you are not mad. All your symptoms are simply due to the neglect and traumas you suffered as a child and are a perfectly understandable response. I was wondering if the voices are stronger when you are angry about something to do with the person you're speaking to.'

'Actually, now I think about it, you're right, but also they come when nice things are happening, like during sex or when someone is particularly kind to me. Occasionally, they come when I'm with my children and I really, really hate them then.'

'So when you are feeling some strong emotions, the voices might be present?'

'Yes, yes, I think you're right', I said, feeling like some problem has been resolved. I smiled at Vida as I walked out of her lovely, cosy room and when the voices next appeared in my head I asked myself what I might be feeling and, although the voices tried to drown my reasoning out, I did begin to understand that I could control them.

My strange state receded as my counselling course ended and I was taken on as a bereavement counsellor. I was determined to get my career restarted and earn some money. The counselling was well managed, with monthly group supervision, and gave me a feeling of being part of something rather than feeling like the usual outsider. I found the one-to-one counselling very draining but satisfying and my clients (I couldn't stand this term as it seemed so cold) seemed to be improving, though I had one who seemed to like me too much. Simon's consultancy had been slightly more successful, which allowed us to plan a holiday abroad for the first time in years. It was great to share Sophie's and Adrian's excitement at going somewhere with warm sea and lots of sun. I was starting to think that after the holiday, and when my counselling was more established, I would set a date with Vida to leave therapy.

Chapter 9

The summer holidays were over and I was back facing my warm therapist, feeling very confused about myself and my life, especially because it was nearly seven years since I had first begun therapy. I was asking her what was wrong with me; I had been on holiday in a beautiful place with my family, yet all I could think about was how I wished I was at home. Then, when I got back to work, in a group supervision the other women laughed and cracked jokes about my client, which I found awful, but I didn't manage to defend myself or my client and now I hated that group and didn't want to go back. A vacant silence ensued, then Vida shifted in her chair and began to speak.

'It's important that you can tell the group how you felt about them making fun of you and your client. Do you think, at your next meeting, you could let them know how their behaviour came across to you?' I sat saying nothing, as just the thought of trying to confront the group made me feel panicky and sick.

'But the supervisor seems very close to one of the other women,' I said, 'and I can't think of what I would say to them because they also sometimes joke about their own clients, which I find very uncomfortable. In fact, sometimes it's like a group of gossiping women.'

'Well, that's even more reason to tell them because they need to know that it's not acceptable to laugh at their clients.'

'But sometimes they can be very empathic and sensitive about their clients.'

'That's good, but it doesn't negate the times that they belittle their clients' problems.'

The session was nearly over so I reassured Vida: 'Yes, next meeting I will say something.'

A couple of weeks after this session, I had a dream that completely shocked me, like being hit in the head so hard that I was knocked unconscious to the floor and could not get up; I had been thrust on to a life path that I never could have imagined or anticipated. I ran into Vida's room and threw myself into my chair and, gulping for air, told her of my dream.

'A fat, old, grey-haired man is dragging me towards him from behind. I'm being dragged towards him on my tummy and he's holding one leg in each arm. I am on a double bed, the room is completely dark. I am naked from the waist down (my nightie twisted around my tummy). I am a little girl. As he's pulling me towards him, I'm screaming for my mum. I can't breathe with the terror. I have never felt anything as desperate as this. As he's pulling me towards him, I'm calling for my mum. Nothing but complete blackness. I suddenly know that she isn't hearing me, that she isn't coming. I wake up sweating and breathless and I suddenly know that I was raped in my bottom and it hurts now and I feel complete horror and I want to scream continuously "NO!" until I die.'

I turned to Vida shouting: 'Is it possible, is it possible?' She sat silently, looking at me with such a serious face, and simply nodded her head very slowly. I started to gabble. 'But how? Why? How can a dream tell me? How can it happen? Why now?' I sat in a stunned silence until Vida's gentle voice reached me.

'It's very important that you understand that this has come from you.' I had no idea what she was talking about and I left that session walking like a zombie. I had been catapulted into a mental state of muddled horrific images (which were worse at night), strange sensations in my body and with the strongest desire I've ever had to commit suicide. I could not bring myself to tell Simon and manage to keep a normal face, particularly when the children are around. The only reason I was still there was because, whenever I planned my suicide, I could not bear to think of how my children would survive.

In my next meeting with Vida, the room felt very strange and Vida quickly rushed in with: 'You know that when Freud and his daughter came to England to escape the Nazis, Anna said to Freud: "Why don't we just end it now?" and Freud replied: "Why should we do their job for them?"'

I sat immobile and stiff, occasionally saying: 'How is it possible?' and 'I won't let my children suffer because of what might have happened to me.' I was in a confused and very dazed state and a few days later I woke up with an excruciating pain in my lower back, which was so bad I could barely walk. Simon called the doctor who prescribed painkillers and rest. I started to take regular doses of Brufen as I was determined that I would be mobile, to the extent that I insisted on driving myself to my next therapy session. I was walking with a limp and when in Vida's room asked to lie on her bed (she had a single bed in her room for patients who wanted to do full psychoanalysis).

I was speaking quietly but angrily: 'How could my father have taken me to and from that place and not seen what was happening to us? How could you tell me that story about Freud because Anna had her father protecting her? My father threw me into a place full of the most horrific monsters you could ever imagine. How could he have done that to us?' Vida was sitting facing me, looking towards me with watery eyes.

'I'm glad you can tell me how you feel. You've had a big shock and it will take time to recover. You need to be looked after.'

I limped from my session. The pain was all-consuming and it took all my attention to manage to walk and drive. Half-term was approaching and we'd arranged to go to Scotland for a week and Sophie had invited a friend. I was determined not to cancel; we'd had so few holidays and the children needed it. I kept taking my painkillers and Simon did all the driving. A couple of days after we arrived, my neck began to swell up. I tried drinking lots and gargling but nothing stopped my neck getting bigger and more painful while I was getting more lethargic and ill. We had to go to the local doctor who told me I had a very bad dose of tonsillitis and put me on two kinds of antibiotics. Simon was great and entertained the three children while I stayed in bed for the whole holiday. On our return, I decided that I would have to tell Simon.

'I think the reasons I've been so ill recently is because of a dream I had.' I explained the dream and my last few sessions with Vida.

He sat silently and eventually said: 'That's really bad. Talk to me whenever you like.'

I was stunned by his response because he didn't question

whether it happened so I asked him: 'Why do you believe me?'

He replied seriously: 'I've always known something really bad happened to you and now I know what.'

This was a turning point for me and I stopped having such strong suicidal daydreams and began to feel very angry with the world or God for creating such people. I decided to write down whatever came into my head from that period and send it straight off to Vida without re-reading it.

What are these memories/fragments that come to me? Are they real? Come on, time to get ready. I feel sick. Please mum, come and get me. Why doesn't dad do something? Upstairs, bend over bath, rubber tube in bottom, water in, then on toilet, to clean me out, you must be clean and empty, are you finished? Bath cold must be clean, nightie on. Bed, horrible double bed, massive high, get it let's have a look, open your legs, cream horrible nice feelings, what are they doing? Bend over side of bed. She's ready, man with vest and pants on behind me, open bottom, thing strange, screaming, crying, hurting, smack on bottom, keep still, it always hurt first time, you'll soon like it, don't move, keep still, it hurts it hurts, keep still, smack, keep still. I'm being ripped apart inside, I've got something enormous in my bottom, eh lassie, that's good that's really good, you're a good lassie, over, throbbing, sticky stuff running down my legs she comes to clean me up and puts cream on, won't hurt as much next time, you'll thank me, teaching you about men, we have to do it for them. My bottom is hurting so much, how can it be? My bottom hurts, throbs, stings, throbs. How can this be? What is that? Burning. Burning, burning, burning. How can I feel burning in my bottom as I write this? In daddy's car. 'Daddy, daddy my bottom hurts, they hurt my bottom.' 'Be a good girl and they won't smack you, you've got to be good and look after your brother, your mother is ill.' 'But daddy they hurt my bottom.' 'I've told you, be good and they won't smack you.' 'Daddy please take me home they're hurting my bottom.' Daddy shouts at me: 'Shut up and be a good girl, your mother is ill.'

I arrived at my meeting with Vida, walking slightly better as my back was improving (though I had regular heart palpitations, which I tried to ignore) and, as soon as I sat down, I began speaking fast.

'I obviously tried to tell him but he swept away my attempts to tell him something was wrong by insisting that I be a good girl and everything would be fine. I can remember trying to tell him but having no words to explain what was happening, and can still feel the strangulation in my brain trying to find words. In the end all I could explain was that "they were hurting my bottom". He obviously assumed I meant they were smacking me and persisted in telling me that if I was a good girl they wouldn't do it. I can feel the awful frustration and desperate loneliness and terror at not being able to make him understand. In the end, he got angry with me and smacked me around the face, saying: "Your mother is ill. You have to be a good girl." After this, I gave up and would sit immobile in his car not saying anything and he was so preoccupied he didn't notice. He left as usual for France over the Christmas period with his legitimate family. (This made me feel breathless with agony.)

'Maybe he was a psychopath the way he could completely ignore our plight and somehow value our needs as so very different from his legitimate children's needs. It was excruciatingly painful to be ignored so completely by my father. He could have saved me but he chose not to and I could only feel disgust and rage towards him. He broke my faith in him and it never came back. From this time on, I hated him more than I loved him but I didn't know it. Yet also I feel that he just had no knowledge or understanding of what people could do to children, so maybe he was simply very neglectful and not wilfully malicious.

'We didn't see my mother for the whole three months but Joss visited her with Robert. How strange that Robert, who had left her, looked after Joss and visited my mother, yet my father never visited her in the hospital. My mother was discharged from hospital before Christmas but chose to leave us in foster care until after the New Year. She and Joss went to stay with my mother's wealthy aunt, who lived alone in a large detached house, but she said she could only manage one child, which gave my mum a reason to leave us. My mother tried to console me with the fact that she did go to get us presents, which she dropped off with Joss. I couldn't fathom the cruelty; even if we weren't being abused, to be visited and then left again. The confusing bit for me in relation to my mother is that she did come to take us away; she saved us after New Year and took us home but I also felt the agony of her having left us that extra two weeks and I really resented the fact that Joss was treated differently. I was also stunned that even my mother's family couldn't find a space for us, despite their wealth and comforts.'

I continued speaking, leaving no room for Vida.

'Is this fucking real? All those words I've just said to you feel like they were spoken by someone else. I just can't seem to feel it's real. Do you think I made it up?'

Vida looked at me forcefully. 'Why would you make such things up? Where would these images in your head come from?'

'Maybe I made it up subconsciously to get your attention.'

'I don't think it's possible for the subconscious to make things up and I'm sure you wouldn't be so ill if it was not based on reality.' I left this session fighting with myself inside my head; was it true or false? Voices told me: 'It really happened, how can you doubt the messages from your body.' others said: 'Stupid bitch making all this up just to get your fat, ugly therapist's attention.'

On getting into my car, I put my music on. Since the first dream all I could listen to was rap music and, whenever I was alone, I had to have the thumping rhythms in the background or I started to sink into the chaotic mush in my head; horrific images, painful feelings and random voices. I was still trying to fight it all and continued to go to work (I did have to have some time off sick with my back and tonsillitis) and the group supervision was going better, as I simply ignored any jokes that I felt were an attempt to belittle our clients' distress. However, I was exhausted and told the group that I couldn't take on any more clients because of personal problems. My supervisor phoned me up and told me that she was available if I needed to talk about anything. I let her know that I appreciated her concern but as I was already having counselling, I'd prefer not to burden her. This was obviously not what she wanted because, after this, even though she did her supervision correctly, she was distant and wary with me. Events overtook my resolve to be strong and I had another dream that I desperately related to Vida.

'I am outside on an unsteady platform, held on a tall thin piece of wood in the centre. It's all wobbly and I'm afraid I will fall. I am in a playground, high above a metal climbing frame. I am naked, a little girl, clutching my clothes over my arm. I notice that my little brother is playing, naked, at the side of the platform. He is about three, I'm terrified he will fall and try to tell him, but I'm frightened that if I move the whole thing will fall and my voice doesn't seem to work. He falls. I am terrified he's dead. I am so scared he's dead. I try to look down without moving, in case I fall but see him playing on the climbing frame. He seems not to know he's hurt but there is blood all over his bottom and dripping on to the ground. He's dying and he doesn't know it and I can only watch and do nothing. I think I see my older sister in the distance and cry out, but she just carries on and doesn't hear me and disappears. I stand there helpless, unable to do anything to save him. I feel completely hopeless and utterly defeated and completely alone, immobilised and numb. I wake up feeling that I'll never be the same again, that any hope I ever had has been erased, that I am completely alone.'

I look at those warm, brown eyes. 'Why am I at a playground? How could I watch what they might have done to my little brother?'

'Maybe they treated you like toys and that's why you're in a playground.' I stared at the gently swaying branches of my outside tree with their faded green leaves and picked up another thread from my memory of strange behaviours of mine that began to occur when I was back home.

'I shit on the path outside our back door. It looks huge and disgusting, like a dog shit. I can't believe I have done it. My mother comes out, looks shocked and says absolutely nothing, then shovels it up and buries it in the garden. Joss is giggling behind her and I feel so ashamed. What is happening to me? I am lying in my mother's bed and I have put one of her suppositories in my bottom. I lie there feeling scared and so confused as to why I did it and it feels sore and burning. I cut my hair off at the front of my head right to the roots across my fringe and towards my ears; my mother is aghast and says nothing. I get my mother's bright red lipstick and paint the whole of my face meticulously and carefully so that there is no skin colour left visible; my mother cleans it off roughly. I am lying in bed with my mother and brother and he is punching at her breasts very hard and angrily. She laughs and holds his wrists until he twists away crying. I am lying in bed with mummy because I have tummy ache and can't go to nursery. Daddy arrives and I hide under the covers. He is very angry when he sees me and marches out. I try to cut my brother's hair but he doesn't want me to and apparently I throw some scissors at him. My mother is horrified and brings my father's discipline to bear. My father pulls my pants down and puts me over his knee and smacks me for what seems like an age. I run away and hide under my mother's old bed for what seems like for ever and nobody comes to find me. I feel my humiliation is complete and I want to die.

'Soon after, in a rage, I smash my hand on a table and hit a glass, cutting my thumb badly, which my mother bandages, although it should have been stitched. I wish I could bleed to death. My brother finds my mother's cine films of us (for some odd reason my father was obsessed with taking cine films of us that he never watched) and pulls them out and makes them into an irreparable tangled mess with the boy from next door. When my mother finds them, she becomes hysterical and phones my father. Then I remember standing outside the downstairs bedroom while my brother is sobbing and yelling and my father is spanking his bottom. I want Mummy to tell him to stop but she doesn't. I feel indignation and rage towards both of them. I feel my brother's pain so acutely and would do anything to stop it.'

'Do you think this behaviour indicates that it really happened?' I asked imploringly, hoping that Vida would give me a way out.

'Well, they certainly suggest that you were disturbed, which could be explained by the trauma of what you had recently suffered,' she clearly stated.

'It's so ridiculous because I've read about stuff like this for years in the papers yet I still can't believe it might have happened to me. Why?' I was desperate for some relief.

'It's very difficult to accept that people could treat you in such a terrible way.' Vida spoke very slowly and deliberately. We sat in a deep and soulful silence until I had to pick my body up and take my long walk to the car (it was ten minutes away).

I had moved into a grey and Godless place; I used to think that some sort of God might exist, but not anymore. How could there be a God in such a terrible, terrible world? There's nothing but random events. The only visions I had on my horizon were my children; I would win for them but sometimes the thought of suicide became so strong because I reasoned that my children would be better off without such an ill me. The only relief I had was writing poetry that I sent to Vida most weeks; when my feelings became so unbearable that I just wanted to stab myself over and over, I managed to calm myself with writing. I had only one client at work now, who I saw every two weeks, and I was still convinced that I needed to hang on to the possibility of my career in counselling. The dreams kept coming, though, and at a meeting with Vida I was describing my latest shocking nightmare.

'I am in a crowded room, as the adult me, looking towards the group of people and see a big, tall, grey-haired man carrying a young blonde girl on the left side of him by holding her legs up towards his stomach so the child's head is almost level with his. He is laughing and talking to someone, not paying attention to the young girl in his arms (who looks exactly like me) but she is locked to him and she is looking straight at me. I am terrified, just looking at them. I know something horrific and unbelievable and not possible and not of this world (I can't find any words strong enough to describe this feeling) is going to happen and I can do nothing. As she looks at me straight in the eye, her face becomes featureless, a terrifying face with no eyes, nose or mouth; just a flat piece of nothingness. Covering the left side of her face and dribbling down this side of her face, is some snotty, whitish-looking liquid. I wake up feeling pure terror and horror, particularly at the memory of her dissolving face.'

I was shaking as I asked: 'What does it mean? Why do I lose my face?'

'Perhaps you lost the sense of who you were during this terrible time.'

'Why do I feel burning in my bottom now, when I think of having my babies I don't get the pain?'

'Yes, the strange thing about torture is that the memories are often felt physically, as well as emotionally,' Vida replied in a factual tone.

'But how? I don't understand. Childbirth was excruciating but I can't feel it when I think about it, yet my bottom is so painful deep inside I can hardly sit down when those awful images come, when I talk to you about it and when I write about it.' I was leaning to the side in my chair to avoid the pain while leaning towards Vida, wanting some answers that made sense.

'It's very hard to realise the terrible torture that was inflicted on you by adults.' Vida's voice was very far away from me.

I made my way home and, although my back and tonsillitis had gone, I felt terribly ill; I hadn't slept properly since the first dream and my throat periodically became raw and painful. I also felt very scared of how I might manage without Vida during the impending Christmas break and I asked Simon: 'Do you think Vida would say no if I asked to take her picture?' He encouraged me: 'I'm sure she won't mind.'

I became fixed on the idea that, if I just had her photo with me, I wouldn't feel so bad and in the session before the break I stumbled quickly: 'I don't know how I'm going to cope through the next break and I was wondering if you'd mind if I took your photo?'

'Of course I wouldn't mind. I'm happy for you to have my photo.' I pulled my camera out awkwardly and began to take some photos of her and her room. I fumbled nervously with the setting, asking: 'Did the flash work?' Vida looked at me with pained sympathy.

'Yes, yes the flash worked. I'm sure you've got some photos.'

I rushed excitedly home and downloaded my pictures. They were great and I printed one out and put it by my bed in the hope that her presence might make my night terror less paralysing.

I immersed myself in creating a great Christmas for my children. This was the first Christmas that we received nothing from my sister and we now hadn't spoken for a year. I had more dreams over this holiday and I sent them straight to Vida, feeling that they couldn't hurt me so much.

I'm in an alien spaceship as an adult where they are taking humans and turning them into zombies by taking their life force. I see trolleys of human zombies wheeled passed me. I am terrified that they'll get me. I am sitting at a round café-like table with this old, fat man sitting opposite me. He has a long, sharp, gleaming hand knife. He's going to stab me and there is nothing I can do. He leans across and stabs me in the heart. It hurts like mad and the knife has parasites on that, once in my body, slowly eat me from inside until I'm only a shell. I know that there is nothing I can do and the pain in my heart and chest is deep and acute. I wake up and have chest pain all day.

I am a child lying down in some sort of body brace, in a crowded room full of odd-looking people I don't recognise. Am I on an alien planet or a foreign land full of monsters? I am a child of about five, I cannot move. My mouth is full of some dry food (like muesli). I fear if I breathe I will choke. I need to get up in order not to choke to death. A strange boy or man comes over. He looks like an alien, with strange solid blue eyes. I mumble to him to help me sit up. He laughs and says: 'Oh, you want me to feed you more.' Then he turns around and squats over me and is going to shit in my face. I have one free hand and try to push him away but my hand ends up in his arse, which makes me feel utter despair. He laughs. I can do nothing. I awake in despair.

The Christmas break was finally over and I was sitting in Vida's warm, soft-smelling room staring at her bed, floating off into a fuzzy-wuzzy land. Her voice wafted gently into my head. 'How are you today?' The silence continued until Vida blew her nose loudly and I was catapulted to her.

'Oh, you know, the children enjoyed Christmas but I'm still not sleeping and, when I eventually do sleep, waking up is awful.' I lost myself again, gazing fixedly at her soft bed and I imagined lying asleep (as a little girl) on my side with my back pressed against Vida's soft warm body and her arm across my chest and tummy, holding me safe for ever.

My vision disappeared as Vida asked: 'Why is waking up so awful?'

'Well, for an instant on waking, I look around the room and feel OK, then I start to feel something is terribly wrong. Then the memories of the last few months come flooding back and it's like being told for the first time again and the agonising pain and terror makes me crave for non-existence. I force myself out of bed, because of my children, wondering how I'll get through yet another day with all this abuse stuff in my head.'

Vida leaned towards me. 'It does take time to find a way through such terrible events but you will manage it with support.'

I left that session not really believing that I would ever feel OK again. I became like a robot, moving from one event to the next, only to be revived by my children's smiles, their innocent, beautiful eyes and their warm cuddles. I occasionally connected with Simon but he was very busy working and I didn't want him to be too burdened by my stuff, because he was still wrestling with getting enough work to make his business viable. I felt so guilty not being able to work and earn money but he kept reassuring me, saying I had to concentrate on getting well. I still worried that we might lose the house. I didn't care about myself but I couldn't bear the thought of causing my children any pain.

My writing also kept me from sinking into nothingness. I sent something to Vida every week. That week I sent her a poem.

Retreat

I was really real yesterday.
Maybe your white form was to have me sent away.
I'm in a very deep dark hole.
I have to strain my eyes to see out of it.
I can hardly hear anything from outside.
I float around, marooned and cocooned.

I am in a strange state of non-existence.
Nothing means anything.

I can't understand anything.
It's all a complete senseless mush.
I can hear that song in the background,
Thumping in a stable rhythm,
Same song time after time.
Even when it's off, it's mostly all I can hear.
I am floating in the thumping, cocooned and marooned.

I can hardly write;
My fingers are numb,
My head fuzzy,
My mouth barely moves.
It's such an effort to move myself.
I did go shopping for my daughter's prom dress.
She looks so different, I don't recognise her;
I am her mother, I know I am,
I am her mummy, I will keep saying it,
I am her mummy, I am her mother.
I am floating, marooned and cocooned.

You are my Mummy Therapist.
The only way I survive is to feel you constantly with me.
Always in the background, like the song;
My Mummy Therapist is like the witch of the west
She looks so angelic, and smiles so kindly,
She has big beautiful pillows of soft warm flesh
That cover me, inside and out, with soft warm gentleness.
I am all fuzzy and floaty, cocooned and marooned.

I have never been fed such gentle soft warmth.
I can feel it deep inside,
Somewhere so completely empty,
And so very sore and so severely hurt,
It soothes and makes it better,
Till the hurting comes back and I need more.
This is where I am and I can't move anywhere else.
I am marooned and cocooned.

I was sitting in the familiar warmth, wondering if she'd read my poem. I said nothing about it. She didn't refer to it. I was stuck in a floaty world that I didn't want to leave; it was too terrorising out there. We sat through long, long silences punctuated by me telling her: 'All I want to do is to sit and stare.'

Vida replied: 'Maybe that's what you need to do for a while.'

I was in this zombie-like state for several weeks until my birthday when Simon insisted he buy me a bike. The children were so excited I went along with it all, not really feeling anything. On my birthday he took us out for a family bike ride in the country and it was amazing because, as I was riding, I suddenly felt a surge of delight at the feeling of whizzing along while surrounded by the beautiful countryside and hearing the excited laughter from my exuberant children. I felt alive and I looked towards Simon feeling thankful for his caring presence. I then had two more dreams that I wanted to tell Vida myself (instead of sending them) and at my next session I quickly relayed them to her.

'I am a little girl feeling totally bewildered and I am lying on the edge of a bed in a pitch black room. A man is kneeling doing oral sex to me. I can see the top of his grey head. He brings me to a mild orgasm, then I think: "Oh no, he's going to do that horrible thing to me." He starts to position my legs open. I feel absolutely trapped and terrified. I awake wet with sweat, heart pounding, and feel such disgust that I had some sort of pleasurable feeling. I'm sick with it.

'I am a small girl, feeling utterly confused, looking up at a fat naked grotesque woman in a pitch-black room. She looks like a transvestite with garish red lipstick and blonde hair piled up on her head. She is smiling strangely at me while unwrapping her right breast from a sticky bandage. She beckons me to suck it. I long to feel the comfort of a breast in my mouth but I'm confused because, when it is in my mouth, it tastes disgusting and makes my mouth all dry and sticky.

'I awake feeling so much horror and sadness because I was so young that I wanted the comforting breast yet that woman chose to hurt the young me so badly. Why? I ask myself so often and never get an answer but I feel rage towards that woman for turning something so beautiful into nothing but ugliness and pain.'

I was seething with rage: 'How could they? How can grown-ups do such horrendous things to small, innocent children? You know, they took pleasure in destroying our innocence. I can see the expression of satisfaction on their faces at our bewilderment and confusion. How do people like that exist? How?'

'Perversion is one of the most difficult things to understand and it causes untold amounts of pain.'

'I fucking know that! Those bastards have stolen half my life. I wish I could do to them what they did to me. I would shove huge, long, rough table legs up their arseholes and take pleasure in seeing them writhing in pure agony.' I was banging my fists on the arm of my chair as I spoke. 'It's too fucking much for me, all this. I wish I'd not come back to therapy. I wish I didn't know!'

Vida slowly formed her words while breathing gently.

'It's very difficult to imagine how you might live with this knowledge.'

'I can't fucking live with it! Haven't you heard what I said?' I turned my anger towards Vida. I marched from this session reeling with unexploded frustration and anger. As soon as I got home, I flung myself on my computer and wrote a poem to Vida that I sent to her immediately.

Fuck you

Fuck you,
Yes,
Fuck you
For being so good
At your job.
I said FUCK YOU,
God only knows what it means
But it sounds good.
It gives vent to my desperate feelings
Of being trapped.
Trapped by your
Efficacy.
Trapped by your
Tenacity.

Trapped by your dedication
To your art.
Trapped by your knowingness.
Fuck you I say,
Fuck you I say,
Loud and clear
For all to hear.
Fuck Freud.
Fuck the unconscious.
Fuck to all repression,
That fucks us all up.
Me precisely.
Fucks me up;
All that's repressed,
All that's festering beneath.
You have the vision
That is trained to see
All that repression,
All that's hidden.
Fuck your x-ray vision.
Fuck your cleverness.
Fuck you.

A few days later, I began to feel panicky at the thought of Vida being angry with me and I wrote another poem for her, hoping that she would be there for me at our next meeting.

Sorry

Please forgive me
For being so angry at you.
I didn't really mean to say those awful words
In relation to you.
You have shown me what real care is;
This is the only reason I can fight them,
This is the only reason I can give a life,
To those who have a right to it.

Please forgive me
For screaming and yelling at you.
But you make me see so much, too much,
Though I know you take things carefully.
It's too hard to see it all,
My extenuating reasons are
That people have been mostly injurious to me,
Then so often indifferent
To my pleading for some love and care.

Please don't leave me;
I still awake in cold fear, not wanting to know of what,
Willing myself back to sleep, till the light appears.
When will this recede, when will I be allowed to move on,
To leave all those monsters behind?
I am leaving it to you, I trust you to lead me out,
Just as gently as you lead me in.
I trust you, I now trust you.

Please don't leave me,
Because I haven't been able to tell you,
Because I don't know how,
But my respect for you has grown.
My admiration for you is accumulating,
Each time we meet and you are there,
With your real listening and real seeing.
I will keep arriving till it's over
And I will keep leaving till it's finished.

I walked slowly into my next session, looking worriedly towards
Vida. I felt such relief as she gave me one of her widest and
warmest smiles. I immediately began to speak.

'I'm a fucking mess. I've lost the few friends that I had because
I haven't bothered to return their calls since I had those first
dreams. My work has almost ground to a halt; I see my one client
every two weeks, occasionally cancelling due to my illnesses, and
we've set the date for the last session and I don't think I can do it
any more because I have no hope to offer them. I sometimes go to
my supervision but say as little as possible and the others have

stopped trying to be friendly with me. I hardly speak to my mother because I never phone her (she manages to call me monthly). The only person who knows about the last ten months is Simon. We also hardly see any of his family.'

Vida looked at me with pain in her eyes.

'Well, I had been wondering if you might consider some group therapy. It might help you to talk to others with similar experiences.'

I was slumped and said in a flat tone: 'Yeah, if you think it might help me, sort it out. When would it be?'

'These referrals can take time, so possibly six months or perhaps a bit more,' she told me, in her most parental voice. I was disappointed.

'Oh, well, I'll just have to wait then.' At home, I was more enthusiastic as I talked to Simon about how group therapy might help me to put my past behind me and finally allow me to manage to have a job and friends.

Chapter 10

The summer holidays were imminent and I'd arranged for us to go camping for nearly three weeks in France and Spain. It was such a relief to be driving far away from all the horror I was facing, I felt it disappear the further we got away from our house. Our children were such a delight and I was carried along by their enthusiasm and excitement. Simon was great at walking endlessly around the ferry with them both. Once on the campsites, Simon was very happy, spending all day with them at the beach and I tended to either sunbathe or swim gently up and down the shoreline. I wasn't very good at playing with my children; I would soon become distracted and distant from whatever game we were playing. As the return approached, I developed another bout of tonsillitis (I had found vitamin C stopped me needing antibiotics) and spent our last few days in bed reading. I felt heavy-hearted returning home and tried to keep alive the positive memories from my holiday and on my first meeting with Vida I enthusiastically shared those times with her.

'It was quite a different experience this holiday because there was a difference in how I felt on the beach in my bikini; I used to be constantly aware of my body and hated men looking at me but this holiday I was able to relax and I wasn't bothered if I was looked at. I even managed to stare back at a man without blushing or cringing. I also seemed to taste food more vividly; I ate endless *tartes aux fraises* and I was able to relax more in restaurants (I used to be so aware of people possibly looking at me eating).'

I smiled towards Vida. 'It's as if I've been sort of numb in some way.' Vida returned my smile.

'You are now free to enjoy the pleasures of your physical body.' I was slightly embarrassed.

'Actually, I wasn't going to tell you, but I managed to have sex with Simon for the first time since all that shit happened and, you're right, it felt much deeper inside me. Sort of not just surface feelings, though I still wish that we could have sex more spontaneously. It's as if we have to plan to do it.'

'Well, it's early days and I'm sure that, now things are better for you, there is a good chance they can improve more.' Vida was beaming with joy. I left that session feeling brighter than I had for a very long time. Unbelievably, yet again, I was to be thrown into a path that would nearly finish me and, as usual, it came via a dream, which I sent immediately to Vida.

I'm a very little girl in some horrible filthy public toilets, in a cubicle with Ray (at about three years old). I seem to know that a murder and rape has been committed years ago in the next cubicle. Ray knows about it and I try to get Ray to tell me what happened while reassuring him that it wasn't his fault. He can only communicate with me using hand gestures to show me what happened. He shows me his hands holding something and plunging, in a downwards motion, into someone. We leave, me holding his hand and I am so angry and just can't believe how despicable some humans can be.

I wake up feeling so hopeless and frightened, I despair of the things that can happen in this world. I just wish I was dead, that I'd never been born.

I was sitting facing Vida, talking slowly and deliberately: 'Do you think the dream meant a real murder happened or could it be symbolic, like my brother and I were murdered psychologically? I mean, what keeps going around in my head is the man saying about us, "these ones are not to be marked", implying that others could be marked. I did have that dream about me in his arms in that group and I was so terrified of what was going to happen.' Vida was very alert as she quietly tried to answer my question.

'Well, I don't know what your dream means because the interpretation is dependent on what feels right for you. Only you can tell me what your dream means.'

'But that's the fucking point! I don't know what it means. I do know it scares the shit out of me. I mean fear like you could never imagine; complete paralysing terror, even worse than in that fucking first dream. Sometimes I get images of a dead baby but then the visions switch to my doll that was burnt at Summerhill, so I just don't fucking know. I don't want to fucking know but I can't stop the pictures and voices in my head and the fucking dreams won't stop. I wish I could chop my head off and let the blood gush out of my body so it empties completely, then I would definitely be dead.'

I sat rigidly in my chair, almost getting up to leave.

'Yes, you have had a long time with very disturbing dreams and thoughts but with support you will get through.' Vida spoke to me in a firm, holding tone.

I was so exhausted with it all and made my way slowly back home with my comforting, thumping rap music. Over the next few weeks, I was propelled into searching for books on abuse and was horrified to find that on searching 'sexual abuse' on the Internet I was given over two thousand entries. I was either incredibly naive or I had unconsciously avoided possible contact with this subject; I remember that if there were articles about incidents of abuse, I would try not to read them and turn the TV off if a news item was about sexual abuse of children. I also rarely watched TV programmes or films containing any amount of pain and horror; if I did, I would get a racing heart with palpitations. I ordered a few books and, when they arrived, shut myself in my bedroom flicking randomly through them. I would start to read bits and then have to put them away until I could bear to read them again. I was so desperately depressed about what adults could do to children. Worse was the information about biological parents abusing their children and the group paedophile ring stuff was completely horrendous. The books sent me back into a zombiefied state, though I wrote poems and sent them to Vida.

It Happened

It happened, so you say.
Why do I have memories before,
Memories after,
But only had memories recently
Of this 'happening' in between?
I thought it was impossible
When those first images in my head appeared

I thought a body so small
Couldn't possibly take something so huge,
And still be alive
And not be turned inside out
And laid completely bare,
To be picked at by all those vultures.

But, you nodded your head
To my question 'is it possible?'
'No,' I wanted to scream.
'You have got it wrong, you don't know,
You just say "yes" without thought'.
Actually, it's the opposite;
You think so much and so thoughtfully,
That maybe you know more than I do
About what is possible,
About what happened,
About what is inside me.
So, I look to the books;
Please give me the evidence,
Please have the figures,
Please have the facts,
That dispute all this,
That show it's impossible.

But what do the researchers say?
Eight percent were hurt aged two to four,
Thirty four percent were hurt aged five to seven,
Twenty five percent were hurt aged eight to ten.
In total sixty seven percent tortured before the body is
    formed.
Nine percent couldn't even remember when it started,
So how young were they?
Twenty five percent endured 'acts' involving penetration,
Including objects that are far too big to enter,
So they rip and tear and scar forever.
Forty eight percent involved all acts of touching,
And fondling and sucking on fragile bareness,

And all that stuff
Stuffed in their mouths,
Till jaws nearly break,
Till no air enters,
Till it spews into them their sick inducing liquid.
In total seventy three percent of them were totally bare,
In a numerous sample of patients needing a head doctor,
Because of all this inhumane depravity.

But, where in the analysis
Is there anything about terror?
Where are the descriptions of pain?
About all that bodily pain,
Particularly the physical?
No description from their texts
Of burning roaring hot fire coals deep within,
Of open wound soreness buried so very deeply,
Of aching deep inside like never before,
Of bruises all hidden so no one can see.
Pain to sit down, pain standing up,
Pain trying to evacuate anything,
Like shards of sharp glass, are stuck so very deeply inside,
That each movement causes more inside misery
For the rest of our stolen lives.

It happened, so my memory says.
But I only had memories recently of this 'happening'.
Often there was a diffuse sense of dread.
An awareness of a need to search around for something,
That is somehow known, but can't be retrieved.
Yet this is so incomprehensible;
I thought it was impossible,
I hoped it was impossible,
I wish it was impossible.
How is meaning to be made with this?
How can humans be like this?
How can they do this?
Don't we always have a choice or do we?

I was sitting in my usual place, in the soft, cotton-wool warmth of my mummy Vida's room, gazing at the sad, bare branches of my soothing tree when I suddenly asked Vida: 'What do you think to my writing?'

'I think you write beautifully. I mean, the writing is beautiful; the subject very, very sad and painful.' She had spoken a word about me that I've rarely heard. I moved on to tell her of another confusing dream.

'I'm in my house, as me now, in the living room with Adrian and Simon. The house begins to shake and move around violently. It's something bubbling up from under the ground, like a volcanic eruption (I can sort of see it as a black protrusion encapsulating something under pressure, I can feel it somewhere inside me). I don't know if we'll survive. Adrian is sitting in a chair. I put my arms around him telling him it'll be OK (while thinking that we'll all probably die). Simon is behind me. I totally concentrate on protecting Adrian from the truth: that we might die. I cuddle him close to my chest, trying to shield his eyes and hoping he will fall asleep. It seems to go on and on, the shaking of the house. I can't imagine how we'll survive. I am very scared but focussed on protecting Adrian. Then it stops and the house is slightly at an angle with all the furniture messed up. Then we're in a really crowded, dark place. I don't recognise it and somehow I know that my son has died, but it's not Adrian as he is with us (I am so relieved) and am so confused, saying to Simon: "But we didn't have a second son," yet I'm sobbing desperately because a son of mine is dead.'

I was confused and asked Vida: 'Who is this baby that I'm sobbing about? Could it be my brother, or my aborted baby? None of these thoughts feel right.' After a long, sad silence, Vida managed to communicate a few of her carefully chosen thoughts.

'It can take time to understand what dreams are trying to tell us.'

'Yeah, well I'm fucking sick of it all,' I say aggressively.

I left feeling in some sort of limbo, asking myself why it hadn't ended yet. I got my answer a few days later with a dream that I sent straight to Vida.

I'm in a dark room (as an adult) watching the TV, something to do with a baby lying in straw. I want to pick the baby up and am terrified about what is going to happen next. There is a room next to the one I'm in. Ray (about three years old) comes out of it with a sharp knife and I am so shocked. He's trying to tell me something about the knife. He's rushing to me for help. Finally, I understand and can see images of a baby boy, representing baby Jesus, killed by a devil holding Ray's hand with the long sharp knife. There is a baby on my knee and the knife cuts baby's tummy open. I am a little girl.

I wake up wet with sweat and my heart pounding. I cannot take this, I am finished, I can fight no longer.

I told Simon that evening, saying to him: 'It can't be possible, can it? It must be symbolic, mustn't it?'

'I don't know. Some terrible things can happen in this world so I suppose it is possible.'

'No, it must be symbolic. I couldn't possibly have survived something like that without being completely sent mad.' Yet a voice inside me was insisting: 'A real baby was killed'. I was a bundle of panic until my meeting with Vida.

'I can't take this. It's not possible, is it, for me to have seen a real baby boy killed?' Vida replied immediately and very quietly.

'Yes, it is possible.'

'Are you sure?'

I was floored by her loud angry voice saying to me: 'Do you think I'm lying?' I begin to sob.

'But I can't take this. I can't live with this. It's too much.' My hands covered my face as I rocked backwards and forwards in my chair. Vida sounded panicky.

'But you wanted to know the truth. You said you needed to know exactly what happened to you.'

'I did, but not this. I couldn't ever imagine this.' Tears were cascading down my face. We sat in silence until I left and stumbled through my journey home.

I started to plan my suicide, even setting a day. I would drive into the pure, clean countryside and sit on a high place, gazing at the beauty, while I drank beer with an endless supply of painkillers. The day came, I gave my children their breakfast and, as I kissed them goodbye, I nearly broke down sobbing. I knew I couldn't do it. I was back to facing each day in my dead body; waking in the morning re-experiencing, being made aware of the dead baby boy.

I then started to feel a deep sharp pain in my groin (I had had it for a while but it suddenly got worse) with a heaviness in between my legs. It got so bad I had to go to the doctor, who diagnosed a vaginal prolapse, which would need physiotherapy and possibly an operation. I gave up trying to work, telling my supervisor that I was having to take time out because of my prolapse. I was back into being overwhelmed by physical illness and, for nearly the first time, I cancelled some sessions with Vida.

The Easter holidays were a few weeks later and I decided that I had to give the children a skiing holiday. I was in my last session with Vida before our Easter break.

'I'm going skiing with Simon and the children for a week. Well, I don't think I'll be skiing because my prolapse still hurts so much but the children have never been skiing and it's something I've always wanted to give them and time is running out (Sophie was sixteen years old). I remember when I went skiing as a child.'

'It's the Easter holidays and I'm thirteen years old and my father has sent my brother and I skiing in the Alps with a *colony de vacances*. I adore the mountains and, although I love the idea of skiing, the first time we go down a small slope I fall and am too frightened to try again. Ray is a fearless novice skier and, as supervision is minimal, I feel I have to keep a look-out for him. I spend the rest of the holiday watching Ray and the other skiers with envy; I would love to be able to glide effortlessly down the lovely white snowy slope.'

I was lost in a time where I was blissfully ignorant and Vida roused me.

'I'm sure it'll be a good break for you and your family.'

'Well, yes, but it would be even better if my prolapse wasn't so bad. I've been to the physio and am doing my exercises twenty-four hours a day but they don't seem to be having much impact and I'm fed up with it. I feel like I've been ill for so long.'

I avoided talking about anything else and Vida soon said: 'I hope you have a lovely holiday and I'll see you in three weeks' The break soon passed and I was back facing those deep, knowing brown eyes.

'The holiday had been great for the children. They're both natural skiers and only needed one lesson to get them whizzing down the slopes. They were so happy and excited it made it all worthwhile, though I found it really boring sitting in the café taking painkillers for my prolapse pain. Simon went off for short walks. I occasionally joined him, but even that was uncomfortable. I felt like an invalid and hated it. I felt particularly angry seeing other families who were all skiing, I would have loved to be able to do that and when I am better I am going to learn to ski.'

I looked to Vida and shouted: 'I won't let all those fucking bastards wreck my life!'

'Yes, you have a right to have pleasure in your life,' Vida said emphatically.

'I was wondering whether you think it's a good idea, but, I'm sort of toying with the idea of trying to write down everything that comes into my head about what happened at that horrific shit heap of a foster home. I mean, do you think it will help me in any way?' I asked her tentatively.

'Yes, it may well help you. If you start and it doesn't seem to be doing you any good then you can just stop. It's your choice.' Vida was using her softest tones.

In the next week, I sat down at the computer on a bright sunny afternoon and wrote it all out. I did not read it and sent it that same day to Vida.

They started as soon as we arrived. We were told that we were going to have lots of fun. She hugged me pressing her breasts into my face, a bit too vigorously. He ruffled my hair and looked me up and down saying 'what a pretty little thing' and that he was going to have lots of fun with me. They gave us so much attention, I felt quite special and maybe being without mum wouldn't be so bad. They gave us tea, we had arrived late afternoon, and the dining room had a round table looking on to a yard. Then bed time. Woman so excited, taking us to show us our room, two beds side by side, separated by a small bedside table, window at side of beds.

The woman loved to masturbate using us, she loved to masturbate us, she loved to get our little bodies to respond, she got off on it. She would get me to lie down in the middle of her double bed and would pull my nightie up and open my legs. Then she would stroke and stroke very gently in between my legs she would stick her finger in my bottom, so gently, and my face felt all hot and red, such horrible nice feelings. The she would get me to suck her tits. 'Harder, harder.' She even got me to suck her smelly bit and rubbed herself all over my face. Sometimes she would put the stick thing on me or my brother and get us to lie on top of her and she would wriggle about. She loved her tits to be sucked when she was masturbating with her strap-on dildos. Of course little Marian doesn't understand any of it but now I do. I think I had some sort of orgasm, when I was so young. 'See you're enjoying it, just like I told you.' This was often when he was out at the pub, he would come back all smelly and fall all over us and was sometimes sick on us. Once he even shat on me, in the bathroom. He called me upstairs and put it in my mouth when he spat in my mouth I was sick, he was so angry he shat on my face, he squatted over me and shat on my face, can you believe it? Because I can't. I got up and put my head over the toilet to try to get it off. She came in and wiped it off with toilet roll and then gave me a bath and told me to be a good girl and it wouldn't happen again. He never did it again but always threatened but he didn't spit in my mouth again. She said I must try not to make him angry and she put me to bed with a nice bottle of milk. He was always calling us upstairs to do things to us. I had no words to explain it. I told my dad of the monsters; he told me to stop making stories up. I gave up in the end, totally. I did everything they wanted so it would be over a fast as possible.

She loved to make tea with trifle and liver and onions. I couldn't eat. She would force us to eat we had to sit until we finished the plate. That's when she used to get angry, if we didn't eat, especially her trifle. I hate trifle, the squashy sponge makes me sick. One time I was sick. She was mad and locked us in a dark cupboard; at least I could snuggle with my brother. Then she learned that I wanted to be sick so I could be locked in the cupboard so she put him in by himself. I hated that and then I would cry and beg her to let him out. She told me to be extra good and she wouldn't. She always used that to get me to do what she wanted. I would be extra good and do everything they wanted so they would get him out. They learned to get to me through my brother. Then I did everything they wanted, how they wanted.

When is it going to be over? Christmas mum left presents, they laughed at what she had got us. I hate the presents.

Sitting in the living room with my mother and sister, me and my brother either side of my mum, them opposite, making sure we behaved, we'd been told to behave. Woman pouring tea from tea pot. Mummy all strange, she's leaving us, big sister is far away from us, she's walking out the door and leaving us, we are being left here for Christmas, Daddy has gone away, nursery has gone away, we are with them everyday and night with all their friends. I am terrified and I just wish I didn't exist.

If we looked at him in the wrong way he would twist our ears, which leaves no mark but is excruciating. He also liked to grab us under our arms and push his fingers up into our armpits, which is also excruciating and leaves no mark. They would often talk about the fact that there were to be 'no marks' on us because we had to go back. Pulling our hair really hard was another favourite, sometimes he would tickle us and make us laugh but it really hurt. He loved to get us crying and begging him to stop. He used to get so angry with me because sometimes I would not cry, my only defence would be to refuse to cry. 'You're a tough one.' But then there were other times when we were given strict instructions not to make a sound whatever was happening to us.

His balls slap against my bum as he pushes himself into me, slap, slap, slap, they feel clammy and cold, slap, slap. Strange memory, it's as if all I can feel is the slapping of his balls against my bum and I've no idea what it is, it's such a strong sensation. He would force kiss me and stick his fat horrible tongue in my mouth and down my throat, the worst was his stinky revolting thing, when he decided to stick it in my mouth, I would feel like I was suffocating, he would grip my hair with his hand and sort of pull my head to the side and back and stick his squashy stick in as far as it would go and then tell me to suck like a lollipop. He loved to pull it out and wank for the last bit and spray in my face, he would whoop and laugh with glee at how much he had managed to get on my face (he did this because every time he did it in my mouth I was sick).

Sometimes they would line up and all see how much they could get to land on my face, one time my face was absolutely covered, virtually completely, I couldn't even breathe through my nose so I had to sort of shallow breathe through the gunge on my mouth and try not to suck any in as it was dripping down my face, they did the same to my brother. Then they used to find it fun to stick the end of a bottle up our bums, everything was such a laugh. Occasionally the woman would say 'poor things' and take us upstairs and bathe us, but she always insisted on cleaning us inside and out or 'you're not properly clean'. She used to be a nurse so she knew how to make sure everything was OK. 'Don't worry you'll be fine with me. I'm a nurse.' Germoline, lots of Germoline. She would give us our enemas and then use loads of cream to keep us right. She used to put dildoes in us at night, 'it's to open you up love, then you'll enjoy it.' It sort of had straps on that would fit around our waists, very difficult to walk in, we would hobble from the bathroom to the bedroom, it was very difficult to get comfortable in bed as I would feel it push against my back.

The group stuff was the worse, fear dripping down my body, ceremonies, costumes, masks. She's not to be marked; some were there to be marked. In the boot of a car, arms tied at back, tape over mouth, bumpy road, out in the cold, freezing, into an enormous room with fire in middle, on to a big table, legs open, masked man, pumping in me, pushing in me, hurting me, keeps going, holding up some sort of sacrifice. Is it a baby? The scream of the baby is an unbelievable piercing wail and makes my suffering insignificant. Did they murder baby Jesus on Christmas Eve? I am not seeing this. Blood running down his arms, dripping on to floor, put blood on line of people's foreheads, line of men in me, woman standing next to me using creams, back in boot of car, tablets, bottle of milk, bed, she gave us bottles of milk to suck with strange horrible sharp burning taste.

I couldn't believe it. Mummy had come to take us away, for ever. I would be so good so Mummy never got ill again. I woke up at home in the morning, I couldn't believe I was home, I thought it was a dream, but it was real. Maybe I'd had a strange nightmare and I forgot about it. They said if I ever told anyone they would come and kill not only me and my brother but also my mother, sister and father. I knew they could kill. I wasn't ever going to say anything, till now. I'm frightened now that they'll come and get me, even as ghosts. At night I daren't go downstairs in case they're waiting for me.

Were there other children involved who could be 'marked,' did I see other children hurt very bad? Vague images with terror but not clear enough to really know or is it that I really can't bare to know. How would I survive? Yet it's so frightening, not really knowing all of what happened, but also knowing that humans are capable of things consigned to the devil is terrifying. Each day is living within the fear of being taken back and of not knowing by whom or when. Then I begin to reflect that actually I was 'lucky' because I was not to be marked but the others were; yet how can I live with this fact, knowing that I was absolutely powerless to prevent any other tiny children suffering? I also feel now that in comparison to the torture I endured and the torture that was inflicted on other children, what my parents and my family did to me was not greatly significant. It's as if my scales of 'badness' have been completely realigned.

I cannot understand how this torture happens, how do humans become capable of perpetrating such horrific torture? It's incomprehensible to me and I struggle to remain alive because of what they did to me. How can such sadistic and completely hateful (I want to say 'evil' but I fear that this word is too simplistic) behaviours exist? To see someone's eyes with not one glimmer of compassion, just filled with hate and the need to give torture and death is indescribable. How can I live with the knowledge that this really happens? How can I live with the knowing that this might have really happened to me? How can I live with the knowledge that this happens in our world, in our 'civilised' country?

Chapter 11

In writing it down I moved into a different part of this horrible process that seemed to have stages similar to grieving. I was with Vida, speaking quietly and slowly.

'It's as if my whole system of evaluating badness has changed. I mean, I suppose what my parents did to me is nothing in comparison to what happened in foster care. I mean, I'm lucky really, because I only endured three months, whereas some children never escape, so my mum saved my life by taking me away. Should I be grateful to her?'

Vida shifted deliberately in her chair and, in her strong voice, told me: 'It's true that some children don't escape but that doesn't mean that your parents were not very neglectful in their care of you.'

'So I'm lucky and I'm not lucky,' I reflected defeated.

'Well, I don't think it's a question of luck but that, as a child, your parents failed to protect you, which is a fundamental responsibility of parenting.'

'It's all so fucking confusing. It does my head in.' I was now angry and continue. 'I'm fucking alive with all this shit inside me. I have no fucking career, no sodding friends, I have no life outside of motherhood. What the fuck I am supposed to do now? Maybe I should just become a writer and put it all down in a book.' I was shaking.

Vida surprised me by immediately replying: 'Yes, maybe you should become a writer.' I began to laugh.

'But I wasn't being serious. It just sort of popped out of my mouth.'

'Well, maybe you should give it a try and see how you feel,' Vida insisted. I had not seen Vida so enthusiastic about a career suggestion (she seemed to slightly hold back whenever I discussed my counselling plans). I continued to explore my future work. 'The problem I have is we're still broke and I'm worried about the children's future. We have no savings at all, just debt. I know that I'm too ill to work at the moment, so I suppose I could give the writing a try, but it's like trying to be an artist or an actor. So many people don't make it and, the longer I'm not working at my counselling career, the less likely it is to be a possibility. Fuck, fuck, fuck! I'm fucking trapped!'

'It's true that our lives can be pushed onto paths that we might not have chosen but the choice we do have is whether to resist it or to accept it.' Vida spoke in a neutral, factual tone.

'Yes but it's not fair because some people have much more choice than others.'

'Well, that is true and we all have to learn to deal with this aspect of our world.' Vida was still speaking in information mode.

I left the session feeling heavy with the burden of my life. However, I did start to write my memoirs, beginning with my birth. I decided to try to write my whole life in strict chronological order. I approached it like a thesis, planning each chapter in terms of the number of years of my life described and starting with the first chapter. It was tough and very slow-going but it gave me something to focus on and helped me to feel that I was doing something to fight abuse. This pushed me to think that I might try to tell my mother what happened. I didn't really know why but it seemed a good idea and she might have some more information for me.

In my next meeting with Vida, I retreated to staring at the bare branches of the motionless tree framed by her window. Vida shifted noisily in her chair. 'You told your mother what happened to you?'

My head moved slowly round towards hers. 'Yes, I sat opposite my mother and we talked.'

'"You know that during that time with the policeman and nurse I think I was abused" I say jerkily.

'"What do you mean? Did they hit you?" my mother asks.

'"No, I mean, you know, abused in my bottom."

'"What, a big man like that?" my mother shouts and after a short silence asks: "What did it feel like?" Her question renders me speechless and I sit with my mouth tightly closed as she carries on.

"I suppose it felt a bit like when I was a child and the nannies put lumps of soap up our bottoms to make our bowels move in the mornings. You know, it was very uncomfortable and stung."

'I do not pursue this and say: "You must promise not to tell Ray or Joss."

'"Yes, yes all right," my mother says in her usual unemotional tone. We sit in an awkward silence together and my mother says quietly: "I suppose I owe you for your childhood."

'I eventually reply: "Maybe"

'I then get up to leave and, as we're walking towards the front door, she tells me: "You know I wish I'd never met your father."'

I looked into those warm, brown eyes. 'You know, since I was a young teenager, she's told me that and it always makes me feel like she wished she had never had me and it fucking hurts like mad. My own mother wishing that I had never existed.'

'Yes and the soap is not the same as your experiences'. Vida was sitting upright in her chair, speaking loudly and looking very angry. She continued: 'I mean, really, your mother's bad experience with her nannies is not at all the same as the terrible abuse you suffered.' I sat for a while in a pensive silence then began to speak slowly. 'I guess you're right. My mother sort of ignored what I was trying to tell her. Which reminds me of a recent dream.'

'I am at my mother's present house and I'm horrified because she's just had a baby. The baby is in her bed, making a strange noise, and I ask my mother whether it's all right, to which she responds: "Of course." I push past her to have a look at the baby and I see a young baby girl with a plastic doll's head put over her head and underneath the baby is crying. I am really angry and grab the baby, pull the plastic head off, revealing the crying face beneath but her lips are all bleeding as the dolls head had been sown to the baby's lips. I turn to my mother shouting: "How could you have done that to the baby girl?" and I leave her house with the baby, determined to take care of it myself.'

I searched for Vida's warm, brown eyes: 'It was horrible. I mean my mother, who is in her seventies, had had a baby. What does it mean?'

Vida looked directly at me. 'Well, I think the baby is you and she had the baby now because she still does that to you.'

'Does what to me?' I asked, confused.

'I was wondering whether you could tell me what she does to you.' Vida persistently tried to get my brain working but I just stared at her bed.

After some time, Vida expanded her ideas. 'There's something about the baby not being allowed to cry?' I was roused from my floating and the pain was searing: 'Yes, I can see what you're trying to tell me: My mother refuses to deal with my pain, smothering it with her own, and she's done it to me all my life but not any more. I will never try to share anything with my mother again. I'm going to walk away from her.'

We sat together in a deep, close silence and then words tumbled from my mouth without me having really thought of them. 'It's as if my mother has died, yet I feel this happened to me when I was very little and I've only just realised it. My mother stopped being my mother a long time ago.'

'I think to a large degree that is true and I do wonder if she was ever capable of being there for you emotionally.' Vida was using her gentle, undulating tones and my thoughts were running.

'You mean that even when I cried as a baby, she did everything to try to stop me rather than simply holding me soothingly till I calmed down?'

'Yes, that's the sort of thing I'm talking about.' I left the session knowing that, for my own survival, I had to stop trying to get my mother to share my pain. I was feeling very alone and, some days later, I tried to re-establish contact with two women friends by sending them emails, with my poem 'It Happened', explaining why I hadn't be able to see them for so many months. A few days later, I received a long letter from my friend Annabel. She was so kind and supportive and I am still deeply grateful to her. My other friend never responded and, when I saw her some time later, she said: 'I'm sorry I didn't reply but I just didn't know what to say', which made me feel like shit and I lost contact with her.

I began to feel the need to seek out information on ritual abuse because I had vaguely seen, in other books, brief references to this type of abuse. I searched on the internet and got seventy-three results, many fewer than for sexual abuse, but still enough to shock me into facing up to the fact that this was a reality in our world. I ordered an academic book and a book from a ritual abuse support network (both written in the UK). The books arrived and sent me spinning into a very dark space; the descriptions of torture and murder were unbelievable.

I drove fast to my session with Vida. The books were double wrapped in black plastic bags. I had to have black bags and had searched around the house for quite a while until I found them, feeling like I was insane. The only thing that kept me from losing it was praying, 'Please God help me', over and over again. I sat shaking in my chair, shouting at Vida. 'This book, this book has it all in, what was in my head. Listen.' I opened the book and began quoting my highlighted sections.

Children in foster care can also be ritually abused. Don't think because they have no marks on their bodies that they have not been hurt because these organisations have developed many methods of seriously abusing young children without leaving any marks.

I looked at Vida. 'They've used that word "marked". Can you believe it? They've used the same word that has been in my head for so long. Oh God, it must be true! I can't cope with it! It's just unbearable!' I opened the book at another page and read aloud.

Satanism follows the Christian traditional yearly celebrations but turns them into ceremonies involving horrific sexual abuse and murder. At Christmas a baby will be born, out of sight of authorities, for the ritual murder of Baby Jesus. The abusers have masks and costumes and will light fires in which any evidence is burnt at the end of the ritual.

'Did you hear that? The book talks about babies being killed so it must have happened because how would it have been in my head? I can't take this. I don't want this. How is it possible?' I sat breathing rapidly and a long silence ensued until I timidly asked: 'Have you ever heard of it in your work?'

Vida breathed slowly. 'Yes, yes, I have come across this. Not very often, but it has come up in the course of my work.' We sat in a heavy silence until I read from the book again.

I dedicate this book to all those unknown children who are victims of ritual abuse. Some of these unnamed children I have been told about and I have taken each and every one of them into my heart and, for them, the least I can do is to try to make the world more aware of these terrible abuses that go on and on in secrecy.

I looked towards Vida with tears rolling down my cheeks. 'It must be true then.'

Vida looks so sad while softly saying: 'Yes, it probably is.' I had brought a poem that I now read to Vida.

Baby, Baby

Baby, baby I will hold you;
Don't be frightened because
I'll be there to grab you, oh so tight,
And fight with all my might.
But it wasn't enough.
My love wasn't enough to protect him.
They took him from my arms,
Screaming piercingly, breaking any live soul
Then they got the sword of death
And took his precious life,
Not easily, but slowly and painfully.
Horrendous boiling horror and bitter freezing terror
Filled every possible space.

Baby, baby I will hold you tight
All through my life.
I will not forget you;
Your life will be valued by me.
I will shout and shout

To tell the world how beautiful you were.
I will also tell of how you were so cruelly taken.
Your life will always be remembered by me.
Your lost life is being mourned by me.

Baby, baby I'll hold on to you with all my might
Because I loved you and adored you.
You were a symbol of life,
Clean untarnished and sparkling blue eyes,
Soft, soft skin,
Breath like a spring day.
Warmth, warmth you warmed my heart,
Clinging so tightly to my hand.
Your forsaken life is remembered by me.
Does this really help him
And fight them?
Or am I still the naive fool?

Baby, baby I loved you.

We sat together in a humbling silence until Vida had to gently say to me: 'We'll meet again next week, shall we?'

That evening I stood looking out of my office window, seeing the most glorious sunset I had ever seen. It was as if I was experiencing the vividness of the seemingly endless hues of orange framed against the dusky blue sky for the first time. The beauty was painful to see and I stood with tears silently falling from my eyes. How could such beauty exist alongside such horror? I can't cope with the two extremes side by side in my head.

Christmas came and went and my health deteriorated again. My prolapse seemed not to be improving any more. I still had regular bouts of tonsillitis (though I managed to avoid taking antibiotics) and now I was having very bad toothache (my dentist wanted to take my tooth out). Simon found me a good dentist who agreed that it was not necessary to take my tooth out and I had several long sessions of very painful root fillings but I was grateful to still have my teeth and even more thankful to Simon for finding me the amazing woman dentist.

By early spring, I started to feel a bit stronger and I wrote to Vida asking her to return to me everything that I had sent to her. It felt like I was taking a step towards holding it all myself. I walked into her room with my black plastic bag and sat down, feeling panicky. The session moved jerkily along until towards the end Vida asked: 'Do you want all your writing and letters returned to you now?' I blushed.

'Yes, yes, I do.'

She stood up, moved over to her desk and carried a large, brown folder to me and as she handed it to me, queried: 'Shall I try to find you a bag?' I was embarrassed.

'No, no, I have one here.' I opened the bag and we struggled together to get the folder to go in (I couldn't believe the amount I had sent to her), which made me blush even more. I walked quickly from this session to my car, fearing that the bag might burst, and I drove carefully home, thinking I couldn't bear it if I had an accident and someone saw all my writing. Once at home, I put the bag in the back of my wardrobe and I didn't open it for months.

It wasn't until early summer that I was well enough to begin to think about the direction of my life (I had done virtually no writing) and I was in a session with Vida telling her of a recent dream.

'I'm in my present home, dragging myself by the arms along the floor because I can't move my body from the waist down (it's completely numb), going towards the door to upstairs. I open the door and look up to see the huge, long legs of a man. His head reaches to the top of the door and I'm scared but then I realise it's my dad. He sits down on the floor next to me and I beg him to tell me how to move forward in my life and whether I will ever get any of my writing published. He says to me: "You'll not have anything published until you've written the book about your life and you have to write it because it's the truth." As he says the words, "the truth", he hangs his head in hopeless shame.'

I am sitting dejectedly in my chair while saying to Vida: 'I can't imagine ever going back to my counselling career because I feel I haven't got any hope to give any more and I feel that I'm being pushed to write, but it's so fucking hard. I just want to be free of it all.' Vida smiled gently at me.

'I can understand that you want to move on and maybe the writing of it in a book will allow you to do that.'

'So you think that the dream is telling me that I must write my story down?'

'Yes, I think your dream is confirming your feelings.'

I walked from this session feeling that the only choice I had left in my career now is to try to become the writer that I had already talked about sometime ago (in my early twenties I used to daydream about writing my memoir and poetry). I discussed this with Simon and his opinion was that I was already a writer and I should get on with it, though he added: 'At your own pace. Don't push yourself too hard.'

I decided to send my poetry out to a few publishers and a couple of weeks later was surprised to have a reply. I took the letter to a session with Vida and I told her 'I can't believe that an editor would bother to write me such a long letter. Listen to what he says.'

Dear Marian, thank you for sending your poems. They are both moving and harrowing but I'm afraid I can't offer to publish your work. The poems are full of sadness, anger and pain and clearly register the hurt of your bruised self, but I don't think they stand up as poems in the literary sense. The problem I have with poems of this kind is that their subject matter and the telling of experiences are incredibly powerful, and the person's observations, beliefs and thoughts are sincere and honest in confronting such events, but I don't find that force and pain matched in the technique and language (except where you're using jagged, staccato lines). But for me they aren't strong enough as poems, and as a specialist publishing house, the literary quality of books submitted for publication has to be our primary concern.

Poetry, like any art, is a highly developed craft which demands many years of work and practice, and to write strong publishable poems a writer needs to be familiar with the whole poetic tradition, from Shakespeare to modern writers who've been developing that tradition over the past couple of decades.

You've been driven to express your hurt through writing, and that in itself will have great personal value for you, but your poems read to me more like personal testament than poetry. They express your pain and anger forcefully and in a highly literate manner, and that writing down and writing out of the experience must be their greatest value. If you really want to write something for publication, for others, I wonder whether a personal memoir mightn't be a stronger medium. It's certainly one which would reach more readers, and personal memoirs of various kinds (covering writer's own death, the suicides and other deaths of loved ones, difficult childhoods, Holocaust survivors and other kinds of survival) have been widely taken up in recent years. It's just that I don't find your writing works, for me, as poetry (for publication). I'm very sorry that we can't help you, and I hope this letter won't add insult to injury. Best wishes.

I turned excitedly to Vida. 'So I suppose I should just get on with writing my memoir. I mean he did say that I can write well.' Vida returned my enthusiasm.

'Yes, I think that's a good idea.'

I spent the next weeks adhering to a strict routine of writing, in the children's school hours, and housework at other times. However, it was tough reliving it all and in a session with Vida I was depressed.

'I don't see anybody except my children and Simon and I rarely talk to my mother on the phone now. I don't have any contact with my brother or sister or any of my half-brothers and sisters. I just can't understand how my life has come to this. I tried so fucking hard at my career and friendships and I've got nothing to show for it.'

Vida smiled at me. 'Actually, I was going to tell you that the group therapy is to start in two weeks.'

'Oh, I'd almost forgotten about it as it's been so long.'

'Yes, I know, I'm sorry it's been such a long wait.'

I always felt awkward when she apologised to me and I mumbled with a blushing face: 'Oh, that's OK. I hope it helps me to be able to talk to people.'

My mood was lifted while I waited for my first session of group therapy for 'women survivors of sexual abuse,' though I joke to Simon about the name of the group, wondering if they'd have a big sign on the door of the group therapy room!

The day finally came and I felt sick with nervousness. I arrived five minutes before the start and there were several other women sitting and standing in the waiting room. We all avoided eye contact, and I couldn't believe that the psychologists had left us crammed in the waiting room until the exact time (why couldn't we have gone straight to the room and been offered a drink?). At last, we were shown to an even smaller, very cold room. There was still no eye contact and the atmosphere in the room, as we all sat down, was desperately sad.

We had two women psychologists who start the group with the usual introductions then we were given questionnaires to fill in. I just couldn't believe it but some of the questions were like: 'Please rate the severity of your abuse. 1 - not very severe, 5 - very severe.' At this point, I stopped filling the form in and looked around the room. One other woman was sitting looking totally paralysed with pain and was not filling in her forms. We then had a break and all they had to give us was cold water (the room was still freezing). Towards the end of the two hours they gave a relaxation exercise and I had to walk out because being told to relax my buttocks brought back such horrific images and pain that I started to have a panic attack.

I arrived home from the group gutted and at my next session with Vida I ranted furiously.

'How could they be so stupid? I mean, rating abuse! I know you wouldn't ever be so insensitive. I'm never going back, never!' Vida looked shocked.

'I'm so sorry it was like that. I didn't know they would have questionnaires and of course, you mustn't go back if you don't want to.'

I marched from this meeting with Vida still simmering with rage. That weekend, I told Simon: 'That's it. I'm not ever going back to that group and I'm taking a break from seeing Vida.' I wrote Vida a letter, cancelling my next session, and stating that I would be in touch if I needed to see her again. I concentrated on finishing my memoir and then sent the first three chapters to over one hundred agents. After receiving an endless stream of rejections, I finally had some feedback from an agent in a long email.

Dear Marian,

Thank you for sending us the first three chapters of your memoirs. I am sorry to say that we are not in a position to take on any new clients at the moment as our lists are currently full. As I'm sure you've realised, the nature of the industry at the moment means it's very difficult for a new author to get published, and this is inevitably reflected in how open agents' lists can be as well.

From the chapters you sent in, I think your autobiography is a commendable achievement. Clearly your childhood and adolescence were very difficult, and I'm glad to hear from your letter that your life has improved since therapy. Your writing style is fluid and readable and your honesty and memory for detail impressive. Marian's growing determination to make a life for herself outside her home and go to university make her an ever more sympathetic character, an energetic force rather than just a victim.

However, from a commercial point of view I have some reservations about the content. As it stands, the story feels like a list of traumatic events and people who fell short of their responsibilities. For example, the friends Marian makes at school don't stand out as striking individuals. They seem to be in the story purely for the sake of how their behaviour affects Marian. There is some validity to this as the story is about her development, but I think it's something that could be improved.

The structure is very obviously chronological and, in my opinion, this makes the story feel a little mechanical. I got the feeling you had a timeline of events that you were ticking off one by one as you wrote them. Now that you know which events you want to include, I think you will need to restructure these chapters and probably condense them slightly. One way of approaching this would be to organise the story around the characters rather than the timeline; this would be a good way of dealing with the friends problem I mentioned above. As I'm sure you know, it's much more important to give an emotionally accurate impression of how the people from your past interacted than to chronicle their history with absolute accuracy.

I hope you don't mind receiving mixed feedback like this. As I said, there are some very good qualities to your writing and I like how your story is moving forwards. I hope you will continue to develop this memoir.

I wish you the best of luck in your search for an agent.

Best wishes.

I was initially devastated by yet another rejection but as I reread her suggestions, I started to admit to myself that my strict chronological memoir was boring and the detail I included became dull in the extreme. I had often had the thought that a book about my therapy might be interesting but the summer holidays came and my ideas of writing had to be shelved. At the end of the summer, I decided that I would not go back to therapy. I felt a desperate need to try to get a life for myself and felt that my only possibility of work was to write the book about my therapy. I wrote a final letter to Vida.

Dear Vida,

I am writing to let you know that I will not be coming for any more sessions with you. I suppose it was inevitable that I would say goodbye to you by letter (maybe it would be too difficult to say goodbye to you in person).

I'm trying very hard to get an agent to take on my book but so far I've had loads of rejections with a few positive suggestions (some negative ones as well). I am starting on my second book, which is about my therapy and what I discovered. Please send me positive vibes to attract some agent who likes my work!

Sophie and Adrian have done really well in their recent exams and have a full active life with their friends – I thank you from the depths of my heart for this, as one of the most important ways you have helped me is to be 'a good enough mother'.

Well, Vida, I really am saying goodbye to you and I want you to know what a wonderful person you were to me. I will always love that part of you that you gave so willingly to me and you really did save me from a living death and maybe even a real death through suicide or illness. You were a true doctor to me as you have helped me to heal enough to walk into my life with my head held high and my eyes wide open.

How do we thank our saviours? All my words feel like they fall short of what I want to communicate to you. Please don't underestimate what it is to save a person's life. I feel like you have given me the chance to live a real life by helping to free me from my internal prison of being unable to communicate my true self.

With love and affection,

Marian

Two weeks later, I received her reply (almost exactly ten years since I had my first session).

Dear Marian,

Thank you very much for your letter letting me know you do not wish to come for any more sessions. I was very touched by your letter and the thought and understanding it conveys.

It is very pleasing to see how much you have been able to achieve through all of your hard work. As much as I appreciate your gratefulness regarding my help, I do believe that it has been mostly due to your hard work and persistence through the difficult periods. It has indeed been a long and difficult journey for you and it is wonderful to see how far you have come along this journey. It has been a privilege to be allowed to share part of it with you.

I am delighted to hear about your children's success and I'm sure you're very proud of both your daughter and your son.

I will be looking out for your book when it is published and wish you lots of success with your writing and with anything else you choose to pursue in the future.

Since we have not met for the last session to say our goodbyes in person, I just want to take this opportunity to say that should you feel a need in the future to meet to review where you are or should you wish at any time in the future to explore the need for further psychological work, please do not hesitate to get in touch with me or ask your GP to arrange for an appointment for you with our service.

I wish you and your family all the best for the future and do take care of yourself.

With all best wishes,

Vida

Dr Vida Grey

Consultant Clinical Psychologist

The letter from Vida helped me to get through the next difficult months without her; when I felt I couldn't cope or that my writing was awful, I would get her letter out and reread it until I felt some faith returning (loss of hope would often overwhelm me). When I first entered therapy, I imagined it would take three to four years to sort out the chaotic childhood my parents had given to me. I never anticipated the events that probably took place while in foster care and I think that there will always be a part of me that remains in a paralysed silence at the horrors that are possible in our world.